GOD Saved Me
For A Reason

The Story of a Modern-Day Prodigal
and His Journey through Addiction,
Recovery, and Redemption

GEORGE SNODGRASS

WESTBOW
PRESS®
A DIVISION OF THOMAS NELSON
& ZONDERVAN

WestBow Press books may be ordered through booksellers or by contacting:

WestBow Press
A Division of Thomas Nelson & Zondervan
1663 Liberty Drive
Bloomington, IN 47403
www.westbowpress.com
1 (866) 928-1240

ISBN: 978-1-9736-8557-9 (sc)
ISBN: 978-1-9736-8559-3 (hc)
ISBN: 978-1-9736-8558-6 (e)

Library of Congress Control Number: 2020902456

Print information available on the last page.

WestBow Press rev. date: 2/25/2020

"This is the incredible true story of George Snodgrass, founder of the Amazing Grace Recovery Program. From living in the grip of addiction to becoming an inspiration for thousands, George's story is one that had to be told. You'll laugh and cry as you take this journey with him. You will discover his profound insights and be motivated to live the life you are meant to live."—Aaron Lumpkin, author of *Are You Living to Die or Dying to Live? What Will Your Legacy Be?*

"George has been through many dark places as he struggled with addiction. He blesses the lives of many now as he guides people to emotional and spiritual health. The Amazing Grace Recovery Program has changed the lives of hundreds. You will enjoy reading his story of downfall and recovery."—Frank Scott, Ph.D., Director, David Lipscomb University Counseling Center, Elder at Madison Church of Christ

"George's story is a real-life testimony that God is a God of redemption and reconciliation. Not only has George experienced the immeasurable love of God, he has spent his life helping others come to know they are loved and never beyond redemption. Thank you, George, for being a true 'minister of reconciliation.' This is a must-read for those who have been deceived into believing they are too far gone."—Jason Shepherd, Vision and Teaching Minister, Well House Church

"This book details the troubled life of George Snodgrass who ventured into the dark side and years of self-destruction. After many prayers from righteous people and the understanding support of other recovering addicts, George turned to accepting the grace of God that had always been there. For many years through his Amazing Grace Recovery Program, George has provided a listening ear and an understanding heart for many troubled souls."—Bobby McElhiney, Minister, Tennessee Prison Ministry

"The terrifying adventures of one man's journey into an abyss from which there appeared to be no escape as he traveled the valley of death and then with help from an outside force he ascended to the top of the mountain." —Dennis Wright, Attorney at Law

This book is dedicated in loving memory
of Richard Jeremy Snodgrass
(August 18, 1981–January 29, 2019).
Jeremy was a sweet, kind soul
who loved and believed in the Lord with all his heart.
"Go rest high on that mountain in the
arms of the Lord." —John 3:16

Contents

Acknowledgments

A book is never the work of a lone writer. Many people have shaped me into who I am today. I am grateful to each and every one of them for their contributions to this book.

I don't remember God tapping me on the shoulder before the beginning of time and asking me who I wished to have for my parents. If He had, I would have pointed to Harry Snodgrass and Ruth Thorne and said, "I think they are the ones for me." Of course, I did not get that opportunity and never has anyone else. I always try to remember, when I am judging others or not showing empathy to another person because of who they are or what they may have done, that I was blessed to have started out with the right mama and daddy. They deserve endless praise for their patience and support.

I am grateful to my beautiful wife, Debbie, who has to get the Medal of Honor for sticking with me through better or worse. I love you forever.

I'm delighted by the encouragement and support of my daughter, Katlyn, who opened my heart to unconditional love from the first moment I held her in my hands so long ago. You are everything your mama and I could ever have hoped for! The world is and will be a better place because of you.

I am so thankful for my brother, Jerry, whom I terrorized as a kid. I was a bad influence on him as a teenager, but he is now so much more than my brother; he is my best friend.

I want to express gratitude to the little town of Mt. Juliet, Tennessee. What a great place to be raised! Thank you to my school, my church, and everyone who supported me. Thank you, Class of 1975, some of whom have been my friends since the age of six. Thank you, Gena and David Sloan, Vicky and Terry Hulsey, Debbie and Charles Moss, Frank and Margaret Hannah, Ricky and Yvonne Kittrell, Phil and Tania Bodiford, Debbie Melvin, Cynthia Glymp, and so many more for your prayers, friendship, and material support.

Thank you, Steve Locke, my literal partner in crime, for being such an important part of my life, the good and the bad, the insanity and the recovery.

Thank you, novelist Greg Lesley, for your help in getting this book across the finish line.

Thank you, Aaron Lumpkin, for your editorial insights and publishing advice. Thanks to Aaron, Jennifer Orellana, Ken Duley, and Laura Durham for supporting Amazing Grace Recovery during my time of illness.

I suffer from an embarrassment of riches when it comes to friends and people who have supported me through the years. They say it takes a village to raise a child, but with this child it took two or three villages, which include the Green Hill Church of Christ, the Madison Church of Christ, and the recovery community I became involved with in 1983, which has been my foundation ever since. Thank you is not enough to say, but thank you from the bottom of my heart to everyone who has supported me and prayed for me. The prayer of a good and righteous person is strong stuff and causes supernatural benefits because of the One we are praying to, and I am living proof of that. I hope this book tells that story of one who was lost, and because many prayed for him, he was found. God bless!

"But he said to me, 'My grace is sufficient for you, for my power is made perfect in weakness.' Therefore I will boast all the more gladly about my weaknesses, so that Christ's power may rest on me." —2 Corinthians 12:9.

Introduction

I am pretty good at looking at myself from the third person, how others view me, because I have spent so much of my life trying to impress others or being so self-centered that I thought everybody watched my every move. I can only imagine some of the reactions from people who know me when they see and maybe read a book about me. I have been writing this book since 2011, with a short break of nearly dying in-between. It was only in the last few months, as I approached the end, that I mentioned to friends and family that I was writing a book about myself. I finally figured out what I felt: ostentatious! I also know the devil wants me to keep the grace, love, and miracle of my life journey a secret. He wants me to keep my candle under a bushel for no one to see.

This is what I ask of everyone reading this, whether you have known me all my life and were a witness to my crazy existence, or we are complete strangers. Remove my name, the messenger, and focus on the message. Focus ultimately on the Messenger, Who has kept me alive and given me my story and whatever it takes to share. Some may think, "Well, George has finally lost his mind," or "Why is he embarrassing his sweet mama and family one more time?" But I feel I have no choice. As the title reflects and as I have been told since I was a teenager, "God is saving you for a reason."

Don't look at me, but witness the extreme love and grace Jesus Christ has showered me with, how I am blessed beyond measure, and how my cup runneth over! Let this story help someone who is sick, hopeless, and helpless, or so they think. As long as we draw breath, there is hope. There is no other logical reason for George Snodgrass to be sitting here writing his story, other than that a supernatural event has occurred: I have been saved from myself and Satan. And what a tremendous act of ingratitude would it be if I did not share it with the world. I am, as the Apostle Paul said, chief among sinners, and that is why I believe Christ picked him for his special work and message. Not that I am in any way comparable to Paul, but I think it shows that Jesus has a way of picking the most extreme individuals who should be handicapped in some way to carry out His ministry.

As Paul wrote in 2 Corinthians about his "thorn or weakness, I also have to give glory to God for His grace in dealing with my thorn or what at times has seemed like a nuclear bomb in my side! I was possessed by a demon, and yet His grace was sufficient! I was the sweetest, nicest kid, the extreme opposite of whom you would pick to end up with a needle in his arm, but that's what happened. I also got as close to the flame as you could get in so many ways, yet He chose to save me. So, forget who I am and look and listen to Jesus Christ at His best as He picks up a broken man and restores him, even giving him a purpose.

I make money in the real estate and construction business to support my family and myself. That is my job, and God has been good to me in those endeavors, but my calling, my vocation, is sharing what Christ has done for me. If He can do this for me, just imagine what He can do for you or someone you know who is lost.

We truly have a friend in Jesus Who walks in when everyone else is walking out, Who loves us as we are, not as we should be. For Mama: Philippians 4:13 says, "I can do all things through Christ who strengthens me." I am Mama's answered prayer!

CHAPTER 1

My Life as a Child

"When I was a child, I spoke as a child,
I understood as a child . . ."
—I Corinthians 13:11

Looking back over the years at the insanity, as well as the serenity that only comes from God's Amazing Grace (hence the name of the program of which I am a grateful servant), I felt it would be worthwhile to share my journey from heaven to desperation and then to where I am today. It is not my intention to be overly graphic for shock value. I merely hope to reach the addict who is still suffering by sharing my experience, strength, and hope. There is an old saying that "A wise man learns from others' mistakes, but a fool learns from his own." Feel free to learn from my many foolish mistakes and maybe a little wisdom that I have gained along the way.

My family came from Wilson County, located about twenty miles southeast of Nashville, Tennessee, and the mountains of East Tennessee. My father, Harry Snodgrass, was born during the Great Depression in Johnson City, Tennessee, into a family of nine children. The old phrase "Times were hard" would be a gross understatement. My father worked at various jobs doing all sorts of labor, including, but not limited to, hauling milk or bricks and working in restaurants. He did whatever it took to survive. My grandfather worked for Bemberg, a German textile company that employed many hundreds of people in that mountainous region, which was generally not known as an industrial area. It was taken over by America during World War II—spoils of war, I suppose. I can't help but think of the irony in this. The same German people (meaning the German ethnicity, not Nazis per se) who were responsible for many East Tennessee families' means of making a living before the war were the same people we would vow to defeat and succeed in doing so.

World War II changed America, as it did my father's life, for better and worse. The worst parts were all the atrocities he saw evidence of, more than any human being should have to witness. The better part was when, where, and how my father met my mother. Many of my father's buddies were drafted, and, not wanting to be left behind, my father decided to enlist in the U.S. Army in 1943. This led him and many young men out of peaceful, small-town rural America into a country mobilizing for war.

I can only imagine the culture shock of someone who had never been more than a few miles from home in twenty years of living and then suddenly preparing to go across the world to fight the evil Axis Powers of Germany or Japan. Germany, as it turned out, was to be my father's destination via Normandy, France, on June 6, 1944, also known as D-Day. Many of the tactical maneuvers for the soldiers destined for Europe took place in Middle Tennessee, of all places. The training facility was headquartered at Cumberland College in Lebanon, Tennessee, and in 1943, hundreds of thousands of young men were sent there to train because the terrain was very similar to that of northern France. My father went ashore at Omaha Beach on June 8th, two days after D-Day. He went all the way to Berlin for the end of the war. In the spring of 1945, he became a liberator of the Buchenwald concentration camp. He was honored for this later in life by the Tennessee Holocaust Commission and spent the last thirty years of his life speaking out as an eyewitness to this atrocity. His favorite saying was "All it takes for evil to exist is for good men to do nothing." He was a good man doing what he could, so that an event such as the Holocaust would never happen again.

Young men, regardless of war or peace, have always had a desire for the fairer sex, and during their time off from training, my father and his friends went looking for girls. One afternoon they ended up in Old Hickory, a small town close to Nashville. A pretty, young, dark-haired girl was outdoors cutting grass. My father, being the gentlemen he was, stopped and asked if he could help. This chance meeting (though I think it was much more than mere chance) in 1943 began a relationship that stayed strong until his death on April 11, 2012. I can't say I haven't been given a great example of marriage and family life.

My mother, who was Ruth Thorne at the time, stayed here and became a nurse in 1946. My father, who by this time had come home from the war, told my mother that when she was ready to marry to give him a call. Until then, he was going home to East Tennessee. My mother, Ruth, finally called, and, as they say, the rest is history. They were wed in Old Hickory in 1949. My mother still remembers the beautiful cream-colored dress she wore that day. It was handmade by my grandmother, whom we always called Mama Julie. Believe it or not, my mother was still able to wear that dress on her fiftieth anniversary, as my daughter, Katlyn, can attest. How many women can say that?

They lived in Elizabethton and Old Hickory before finally settling down permanently in Mount Juliet, Tennessee. Mount Juliet is located southeast of Nashville and, in 1954, was a very rural town, complete with dirt roads and more cows than people. They bought a small eight-acre farm located near Old Hickory Lake that did not have city water running to it. They both worked at the DuPont factory in Old Hickory until my father got a job at the Ford Glass plant, where he worked until he retired. Being industrious hard-working people, they were able to buy a soda shop and a gas station in the heart of Mount Juliet across the road from the only school, which served grades one through twelve. The shop was called Harry's Sundries, and that is where my parents became active in the community, especially with the high-school kids, because it was the only place in town to get a burger or a milkshake. Even now, it amazes me that they were able to work their jobs, doing rotating shifts, and could still run their business. Harry's Sundries was also where I made my debut into the community. I have known some people from there my entire life. There is a picture of me on the counter in a bassinette. My childhood was straight out of a Norman Rockwell picture of small-town America in 1957.

My grandparents on my mother's side lived on a nearby farm off Lebanon Road, which was the only paved road in Mount Juliet at the time, as well as the second oldest road. Andrew Jackson himself traveled it many times. Mama Julie and Papa played a huge role in my upbringing, especially since both of my parents worked two jobs. Papa was not my biological grandfather, but that was never an issue between us. I was still the apple of his eye. His name was Mac Hackney, and in his eyes I could do no wrong. He was always doing something for or with me, whether it was watching baseball while Dizzy Dean did the commentary or going to the Dairy Queen for a milkshake. I remember watching him do the twist, which was a big fad with teenagers back then. I miss Papa as much today as I did when he died in 1967.

My earliest memories revolve around my family's church, Green Hill Church of Christ. My Sunday school teachers nurtured my love for Jesus Christ early in my life. Back then, I had a more spiritual concept of Christ before I learned about all the "thou shalts" and "thou shalt nots." Ironically, I have come back to the understanding I had as a child in the beginning. I have always had a hearing problem but not in the physical sense. What I mean is that what I heard people say about Jesus and the Bible was not really *what* they were actually saying. Of course, I have heard some people who, hopefully, were merely misguided, but that is between them and God.

However, my childhood was idyllic. I received a lot of love from my family and church, and I enjoyed farm life. We went to church three times a week. I got involved with baseball when I was seven and spent summers practicing or playing at the park. My biggest fan and supporter was my father, and I used to feel very proud when he bragged about how good I was. I even made all-star for three of the nine years I played. Life was simple for me then.

My later interpretations of what was being told to me led to my introduction to guilt and shame, and I finally quit trying to do right altogether. Because I believed I was doomed anyway, I went full throttle in later years. Also, having not been exposed to alcohol, not even casually, I viewed it as evil or the forbidden fruit. I had thought that if I ever took a drink, a lightning bolt would zap me, and I would go straight to hell. Naturally, that did not happen. In fact, what did happen was a feeling that came over me I had never felt before. I discovered that sin feels good, at least initially. Now I tell people, especially kids, that the first drink or joint could very well feel good!

In my early years, baseball occupied a large part of my life. From Little League through Babe Ruth, I immersed myself in what used to be America's favorite pastime. Those were the innocent days.

As I reflect on my life, I can see when my athletic skills began diminishing. It happened when I was about sixteen or seventeen. Not having my father building me up about my talent anymore, I felt a void and needed something to fill it. Girls were starting to play a bigger part in my life, though I had always loved girls, ever since my first girlfriend, Star, in kindergarten. Gradually, sports, good grades, and church no longer made me feel complete. Drinking on weekends and campouts had already started to give me the satisfaction that my former healthier pursuits had provided. I had opened Pandora's box or, I should say, Satan's box. I had found a way to change how I felt, and I started wondering, *If they lied about alcohol, what else were they lying to me about?*

CHAPTER 2

Mixed Feelings and Conflict

"Ever since I was a kid at school,
I messed around with all the rules."
—Rod Stewart

The sense of freedom that a car gave me at sixteen was building the perfect storm of freedom and rebelliousness tinged with immaturity. After getting my driver's license, I *always* wanted to go, no place in particular, anywhere would do, but I felt I had to go. In fact, on the road I still get that feeling of adventure that I got when I was fourteen riding around with the older guys at school or church. Perhaps one reason I changed the way I did was because my life as a child was so sweet that I never wanted it to end. Like Peter Pan, "I didn't wanna grow up." Naturally, alcohol took on a bigger part of my life as I began high school. Access to alcohol became easier through older friends or other parents' liquor cabinets. I began to emerge from my cocoon of church friends and swim out into deeper, more turbulent waters. Cigarettes had already been in the picture from around age eleven because, like alcohol later, cigarettes were easy to get. I started getting mine from my father's desk. I would steal one at a time so as not to be obvious. Stealing and sneaking around were already playing a role in my life. These habits helped push the door open for me to step through.

One passion that my father, my brother, and I shared was a love affair with motorcycles, which started on Christmas Day after I turned thirteen. There were two Honda mini-bikes under the Christmas tree, and I remember how happy I was circling around the yard and the barn. My love for anything on wheels began that day. It is only by the grace of God that I am alive to tell about it. As I got older, the bikes got bigger, and I drove like a maniac while wasted on whatever I could get my hands on at the time. Motorcycles were also the catalyst for getting into trouble with the law.

I got busted with a friend of mine for drag racing before school one day. I was struck by the fear of God when I was called to the principal's office and had to face the principal and a state trooper. Luckily, the other boy and I got off with a warning. I was learning very quickly how to talk my way out of sticky situations, which would later be to my benefit and my detriment.

Motorcycles, oddly enough, also turned out to be the catalyst for more serious crimes, such as burglary. Some friends and I rode bikes to the lake and broke into summer homes looking for stashes of liquor, like pirates raiding a ship. We did not realize the seriousness of what we were doing. We rationalized that these homes were left unattended for most of the year, which therefore made them fair game. Of course, the law simply identified it as burglary, which is a felony. The thrill of getting away with a crime was part of the rush that accompanies addiction—at least, it was for me. Having willing accomplices made it easier and more fun. The adrenaline rush that accompanied my feeling of getting away with something I knew was wrong was very strong, but it was also very twisted. A normal person would be morose with shame for going against his morals and values to commit a crime, but most addicts are simply not wired that way while they are in the grip of their disease. What should cause spiritual pain turns into morbid pleasure. The proverbial *monkey on your back* is not only a trickster who tells you not to worry about any possible consequences, but it is also very hungry and demands to be fed until it becomes a King Kong–size gorilla, with the capability to devour you.

I can finally see how out of place I actually felt, leaping out of the Norman Rockwell world I'd been reared in. I had been a good baseball player, active in church and school, blessed with lots of friends, and loved immensely by my family, only to fall into a different world that centered around drugs, alcohol, degradation, misery, and despair. I had everything going for me, yet I felt so alone. At the time, I thought everyone felt out of place or different, and I'm sure many did. My main problem was that even though I had evidence to the contrary, I was always afraid I didn't fit in. I wanted to be cool like Fonzie from the show *Happy Days* but felt more like Toad from the movie *American Graffiti*.

I also had that insecurity with girls. I never felt like I measured up to the guy who always got the girl. I was measuring my insides with people's outsides. For one thing, as a boy of thirteen I had a very high-pitched voice, and other boys picked on me for it, which fed my low self-esteem. They didn't really do it in a mean-spirited way, so I wore it as a badge of honor. After all, being noticed by the older "cool" guys meant a lot to me; any attention was better than none. They let me tag along with them, and I felt good even being the butt of jokes because at least it was from those I admired.

Hanging out with the older crowd also led me into situations ahead of my time with sex and drugs. My maturity level was high in some ways, but in other ways so was my naiveté (though later that would rapidly change). Fast friends lead to fast times, like the Eagles' song "Life in the Fast Lane." It is somewhat ironic that those same friends who lightheartedly (to them, at least—I really don't believe it was malicious) teased me then are still my good friends today. They would even come to my defense shortly after that.

First, I need to digress a bit to explain yet another conflict within me, although it was all probably part of one huge conflict. A Gospel meeting was held at my church during the summer when I was thirteen. I had wondered for some time when I would be ready for baptism, and it turned out that this was the time. I knew baptism was supposed to happen when I was mature enough to know right from wrong and old enough to be held accountable. Part of my motivation was peer pressure. A couple of older friends were doing it, so I decided to join them. I had played ball with them and was picked on by them, so naturally I looked up to them and wanted to be like them. It was at least as much about "them" as it was about me. Though I was younger, I was mature concerning spiritual matters, so I felt confident that I was making the right decision.

This was the beginning of the strange dichotomy of my life: striving to live for and serve Jesus Christ but also starting to drink, smoke, and act out sexually. Bill Clinton had been accused of being able to compartmentalize his life between his political achievements and his womanizing. I can relate to that because I was doing the same things as a young teenager. I became a chameleon, able to change colors to fit my surroundings. At church I was a good kid, but around my rowdier friends I could drink and curse with the best of them. A split began to form in my personality, which widened as harder drugs came into the picture. Drug addicts inhabit parallel worlds until finally they must give up one or the other. As my friend Richard used to say, "It's hard to be respectable and high at the same time." I have found that to be true. If I had known where I was heading at thirteen or fourteen, I probably would have committed suicide. After graduation, my life switched from the best of times to a living nightmare.

CHAPTER 3

I Refused to Listen to God or Anyone Else

"No stop signs or speed limits,
Nobody's gonna slow me down."
—Bon Scott

My early use of alcohol was basically like that of any other kid who experimented with it. Once I chose to leave my idyllic childhood, I decided to grow up all at once—though we all know it does not work that way. After all, I was just doing what a lot of other kids in ninth and tenth grade were doing. The difference was that I was an addict. I drank, felt great, got sick, and couldn't wait to do it again. Addicts are wired differently than normal people. If normal people drink and have bad experiences, they don't have the desire to rush out and do it again the next day. Though they may continue to drink, they do so with caution and moderation.

Moderation is not in an addict's vocabulary. I have never enjoyed "a" beer or "a" cocktail. Once I had the first drink in me, it was all about the buzz, drinking as hard and fast as I was able. I drank more liquor than beer because the old saying is true: "Liquor is quicker." If I drank beer, I would drink it so fast that I vomited so

I could drink some more. We also used to shotgun beers, which is where you poke a hole in the can, put your mouth over it, and then pop the top so it races straight down your throat and to the brain. I did not drink to savor the taste; I wanted to get drunk.

This was about the time when copy machines became available in places like the public library, and because Tennessee did not have photo licenses yet, it was fairly easy to make a fake ID. It was good enough to buy liquor in Old Hickory and some markets in Nashville. The ID was even good enough to get me into some nightclubs. These "dens of iniquity" were a long way from my innocent background, places I had formerly only seen on TV or in movies, dark mysterious places with loud music and women twenty-one or twenty-two years old. Again, as I tasted a bigger bite of the forbidden fruit, I was not struck down! Instead, God showed me His grace by not giving me what I deserved.

By this time I was experiencing blackouts, driving drunk, and going to places I had no business being, but alcohol has a cunning way of making one feel bulletproof. I was unaware of how stupid I was behaving. Thankfully, I had friends who would take away my keys and throw me into the back seat. I was a danger to myself and society. Again, it was only by the grace of God that I did not kill or hurt anyone other than myself. I know many others like me who ended up crippled or dead, or they destroyed other people's lives, but I was too young to know that it could very well happen to me.

One night there was a horrific accident near my home. Two of the three people involved died after hitting a tree while trying to navigate a sharp curve. They drove the same type of car I drove: a Ford Pinto. When I heard how fast they were going, I did the same thing—only I was successful, if you can call that success. Tempting fate became a pattern with me. Of course, I had superior driving skills, or so I thought. Somehow, during my high-school days of being drunk and driving cars and motorcycles like a maniac, I made it through unscathed, but later that would change.

The physical effects of my destructive actions did not appear early on, but the mental effects began to appear quickly because I did something almost daily that went against my nature. I had a well-developed conscience by the time I started drinking, so every time I drank, lied to my parents, or did any number of other things that went against my conscience, pieces of my insides were being chipped away: tiny pieces at first, larger ones later. It was a slow process that that over the years took a big toll, but every time I moved further toward destruction, it became harder to turn back. I was not aware of the slippery slope I was on, even though I knew I was doing wrong. Still, it was also fun. In fact, doing something wrong and getting away with it was part of the fun. I enjoyed the freedom that drinking gave me. I was no longer hemmed in by inhibitions, which had warned me against doing what I knew was wrong. Also, I finally felt like I fit in, whether it was an illusion or not. I finally felt I was "cool," especially because I was in with the "cool crowd." What some kids won't do to be accepted!

During this period, while my old self was rapidly splitting from my new self, I did not realize what was happening, though a lot of others did. Early in my addiction, I was able to keep my "priorities" separate: going to school, getting good grades, attending church, and then partying like crazy with my friends when those other obligations were done. Ironically, many of my drinking buddies were merely experimenting with new things, as normal teenagers will. I was the one out of control. Most of them outgrew the adolescent stuff and went on to lead normal, productive lives. They would mature and have wives, families, careers—all the blessings that go with adulthood—but not me. I had a different path to follow, which got much darker before I was able to emerge into the light.

When my father discovered I was drinking, sometime during my high-school years, he warned me that I already had two strikes against me. What he meant was that alcoholism ran on both sides of my family through uncles, aunts, cousins, and so on, and that if I continued to drink, I could very well end up like them. Of course, his admonition fell on deaf ears because I was too smart for any of that to happen to me. I was merely having a good time, unable to see that there would be dire consequences down the road. Even then, I was in the grip of something far more powerful than me.

I was sixteen when I got my driver's license and my first car, a 1963 champagne-pink Mercury Comet. It had a six-cylinder engine and an automatic transmission and only cost three hundred dollars. Most important, it was my ticket to freedom. I was finally able to come and go as I pleased without being dependent on anyone else. I was able to go to school or work, which included hauling hay and working at the local feed store. It was my space and mine only. I could smoke cigarettes, drink, and do whatever I felt like. That feeling of independence was a rush in itself. I have always wanted to be the one to drive, a habit that has carried over to the present, especially with family and friends. I suppose we all have our own little control issues, and that's one of mine.

I have always been a safe, conscientious driver, if I was conscious of driving. Sometimes, being under the influence will make one forget that one is operating a potential death machine. However, my first *near* car accident happened when I was sixteen, showing me how easily a tragedy can occur. I have always had girlfriends (romantically) and girlfriends (in the platonic sense). At the time of my first near wreck, I had five girls in my car. We were leaving school in the afternoon, and I pulled out in front of a tractor-trailer. I was glad to be out of class, which, coupled with being sixteen and riding with five girls, made me somewhat unobservant. At the very last minute, I realized what I had done and, in the midst of the chaotic noise of five girls screaming, was able to swerve and avoid hitting the truck. I believe God was trying to get my attention, and yet again, it was only through His grace that we were spared. For the most part I became a more conscientious driver, though drugs led me to many more near-death experiences. All that time God was looking over me, and I thought that I was either above getting killed or extremely lucky. Deep down inside I knew the truth, but since I'd begun taking His grace for granted, I did not wish to be reminded of it.

Driving sure improved my love life. I was able to fall in and out of love in the time it took to get from one girl's place to the next. Don't misunderstand me, I was still a decent guy concerning girls. I treated them with respect, but that can be frustrating at times. Sometimes being a "good guy" meant I did not get to go all the way. "Good old George" wanted to be bad, but some things, such as treating women like ladies, can hold you back. Adding to this frustration was hearing how much my friends were having sex. Of course, their bragging was very much exaggerated, which I know now, but at the time I took it for the gospel truth.

The inadequacy I felt only fueled the fire to get drunk, even though the fire was already raging and did not need any more fuel. When I was drunk, I didn't care how awkward I felt around girls. Looking back, though, I am truly glad that this part of my social life was not successful because I remained friends with the girls I dated and did not take advantage of them. I had enough regrets later to deal with, but at least I was spared that one. The innocence of my high-school romances is something I still cherish and a priceless commodity that I did not fully appreciate until later.

During the early to mid-seventies, there was an exodus or migration of sorts from what were considered the "drug-infested" streets of Nashville to the so-called serene, laid back, country life of Mount Juliet. Though there were several reasons for the exodus, a lot of it stemmed from concerned parents who thought a geographical relocation would keep their kids away from drugs—although by then it was too late. It was not a major relocation because Mount Juliet is only about a half hour's drive to downtown Nashville. Basically, the Mount Juliet kids got turned on to drugs, rather than alcohol, by the city kids who came to town.

CHAPTER 4

Rationalization Is the Name of the Game

"Fearing not I'd become my own enemy
in the instant that I preached.
Good and bad, I preached these words as if a wedding vow.
Oh but I was so much older then, I'm younger than that now."
—Bob Dylan

In 1971 and 1972, it was easy to see who was doing what, as far as drugs went. The kids who got high and had long hair and obligatory bad attitudes, really stuck out in Mount Juliet. It was amazing to see over the next couple of years how many different cliques of kids were doing the assortment of available drugs then, from marijuana to heroin. The jocks and the "free spirits" eventually coalesced or at least coexisted. They may have looked different and partied in different places, but they did have one thing in common: they all liked to get high. Choose your poison.

During my freshman year of high school, my life took a strange and ironic turn. Though I was drinking and smoking cigarettes, I drew a fictitious, self-righteous line between alcohol and marijuana or anything stronger. I even took it so far as to preach my views to anyone who would listen. I became somewhat belligerent about it, so naturally the rumor started to spread that I was a narc. I didn't even know what a "narc" was, nor would I have been one if I'd had the chance. I just had a big mouth. One thing led to another, and before I knew it, I heard that a couple of the longhaired representatives were going to kill me. That probably never would have happened, though I most likely would have gotten beat up. I was scared to death!

Thankfully, some of my older friends learned of the situation and told me to stay in class after school one day. Almost like a scene from a movie, a gang of jocks and friends from the country came marching up the hallway, led by Rod Duffel and Jim Sanders. Rod played football and looked like a blond Hercules. Jim was a cool country boy who ended up becoming a lifelong friend. I felt like a million bucks! That event not only kept me from a beating, but also boosted my self-esteem. I was escorted safely past the longhaired crowd, and even though they were high, they were not crazy. The matter died down, as word spread that I was cool; I just had a big mouth. The biggest irony was that those same free spirits turned out to be my biggest drug buddies later on. We laughed about how different we were then and what we became shortly afterward. You never know where life is going to take you. We took an odyssey from being almost enemies concerning drugs to being drug buddies, to being in recovery.

Seeing the stereotypes of drug pushers on TV who lure people into dark alleyways to get high always amuses me. Although this may happen sometimes in big cities, that's not how it happened with me. Peer pressure is very persuasive, even though my friends did not hound me to get high. When you see your friends getting high without having disastrous consequences, it's easier to do what they do. These were the same good old boys I played baseball with and friends straight off the farm. How could it possibly be wrong if they, who were just like me, were doing it? It is much easier to do wrong when those you know and love are also doing it. Word of mouth has always been the most effective form of advertising. As they say, "The devil wears a red dress," though in my case it was usually a John Deere ball cap or a baseball uniform.

Knowing that I was doing wrong, I began a habit of setting dates for when I would change my behavior: the next ball season, my next birthday, or the next school year. Even though I kept drawing my line in the sand and was determined to stick with it, these dates came and went and nothing changed. I had this idea that if I drank but didn't smoke pot, I would be okay. I would be safe by sticking to alcohol. This gave me the illusion of self-control and the feeling I was somehow superior to the dopers. However, I was rolling downhill and picking up speed as I went.

In 1974, I got a job pumping gas at a service station. This was before self-service had come along. I also performed other odd jobs like changing oil. While working there, I met my first functioning alcoholic. He was Japanese and a regular customer. What stood out about him was that he drank whiskey mixed with Dr. Pepper all day long. He was a general contractor who worked for himself, so he had some freedom, but he never let alcohol interfere with his business.

That job was my first employment away from the farm and the folks from Mount Juliet who owned businesses, so it was my first exposure to the "other world." The guys who owned and ran the place were not much older than me, but they seemed to be a lot wiser and more mature, to my sixteen-year-old mind. We drank Miller ponies during work hours, which was looked upon as normal (to abnormal people, at least). I'm pretty sure some hot merchandise passed through there as well, though I was kept in the dark about it.

I felt like a man doing a man's job: cursing, telling dirty jokes, and horsing around—things that men do only around other men. I was driving a 1965 canary-yellow Chevy Impala with factory mag wheels and Michelin radial tires. It was a real head turner that fit right in with my work environment, which was centered on hot rods, and we had one of the best mechanics in town.

I soon learned there was pot around, although I didn't find out how much until later. They were dealing, and eventually I made it up to their apartment. I remember it like it was yesterday. They rolled some joints, and we proceeded to get wasted. I was as high as a kite, and the next thing I knew I was prowling through their kitchen in search of something to eat. It being a bachelor's pad, there was not a big selection, but I found a pack of hot dogs and shoved as many cold ones as I could fit in my mouth. They laughed at me, of course, and I'm sure I looked ridiculous. It was a school night, and I knew I had to get home, but I was too high to face my parents. I drove down to the lake to get myself together. I parked and put in an eight-track tape of Lynyrd Skynyrd's first album, *Pronounced Lenerd Skinerd*, and listened to "Free Bird," the ultimate Southern classic, only then I really heard it. Music had already become an important influence in my life, and although my introduction into the drug world was kind of scrambled, that night sitting at the lake was pretty cool.

I knew I had really blown it by smoking pot. Since I had crossed yet another line I had sworn not to, I used addict logic (which is not logical at all). Instead of turning off the path I was on, I kept going, picking up speed as I went. I was consumed by guilt and shame, while at the same time I couldn't wait to do it again. Getting high was the only way I could try to outrun those relentless demons. Because I couldn't put the genie back in the bottle, the best I could do was run harder and faster, though I could never run quite fast enough.

My senior year of high school is like a blurry kaleidoscope; the main pictures are of me having fun, getting by in school, and partying a lot. Drinking was by then a regular habit before school, and going to class with a buzz enabled me to play the role of the class clown. In fact, drinking and smoking pot became the main focus of all my activities, whether it was Friday night football, school dances, riding the roads with friends, or going to church. I'm embarrassed to admit that I even got high before church on Wednesdays and Sundays with a deacon. I would like to blame it all on the devil, but we are gifted and cursed with God having granted us free will. After church, we got the munchies and went to Shoney's Big Boy, where we gobbled down hot fudge sundaes. I was having fun and started not to be too concerned about right and wrong. After all, if so many people whom I considered in the mainstream were doing it, how bad could it be?

Rationalization played a major part in my addiction, as it would for many years. I convinced myself that I was doing fine, and I certainly didn't go around asking other people who might have told me the truth about myself. In fact, I avoided anyone who wasn't doing what I was doing. I gravitated instead toward those who were. It wasn't until years later that people told me how out of control I really was, especially that last year of high school. I merely thought I was having a good time and not hurting anyone else. That's why I tell people now, young and old, that if they are close to someone who is obviously out of control, confront the person, and do whatever it takes to get his or her attention. It's too late when you are standing around the funeral home, wishing you had said or done something that might have kept friends from ending up dead before their time.

Denial is the first and probably most stubborn symptom of addiction, and the last person to let go of it is the addict. The addict's family will also likely be in denial. There's a huge comfort in denial because it's much easier to blame the crowd the addict hangs out with than the addict himself. I don't remember anyone saying anything to me about my insanity, although they may have, and I didn't want to hear it. Watching someone self-destruct is like watching a car wreck in slow motion. You hope the person survives, but you know reality may paint a different picture. In my case, *only* the grace of a loving God made the difference. The prayers of many righteous people, especially my mother, were being offered up for me, and as the Bible says in James 5:16, "The prayers of a righteous person are very powerful."

By the time my senior year came to a close, life had become one big party. The FFA (Future Farmers of America) had played an important role in my school life because agriculture classes were my favorite. I had even gone so far as to travel with other agricultural officers to the University of Tennessee to see about attending college there. UT was known for its agricultural studies. But that was when I still had dreams, and that dream quickly faded. I was even elected FHA (Future Homemakers of America) King and Sentinel in the FFA, and one of my roles as sentinel was to recite a line at the beginning of our monthly meeting, only I was too drunk to recite it. I was whisked away and somehow managed not to get into trouble over it, but I was ashamed of myself, especially since the incident occurred in front of Mr. Willoughby, one of my favorite teachers.

One other senior year escapade sticks out in my mind: a day when I was too drunk to make it from the parking lot to my first class. Drinking before class had become my routine by this point. I was so drunk that I had a real problem staying on my feet. I was sliding down the lockers when a coach spotted me. Big trouble, one would think, but not in this case. During that time, the kids were partying with some of our teachers, especially those who were not much older than us. The result was not suspension or expulsion. The coach just laughed and told one of my buddies to get me out of there.

The message I received was: *Go on, George, party hard! Make the most of it while you can because you're gonna have to settle down soon, but not just yet.* It may sound like my only friends were party animals like me, but I also had friends who were heading in the right direction. They were planning for the future, going to college, or doing what it took to be successful. However, I had drifted so far that I was simply lost.

On graduation night, there was a positive vibe in the air on the football field. We all whooped and hollered, clapping buddies on the shoulder and getting phone numbers, with promises (that were seriously intended) to keep in touch. But when it was all over, and everyone had drifted away, I cried as I made my way slowly through the parking lot toward my car. I knew deep down, where I did not like to venture, that the best carefree days of my life were over. I was terrified because it was time to grow up, and, above all else, I simply didn't want to. While many of my friends were preparing for the future in a positive way, I was also preparing for the future, one in which I did not have to mature or "grow up."

My future revolved around a world of chemicals, where I could suspend reality indefinitely and become the great pretender. I was the star of my own movie! It started out as a light-hearted romantic comedy but evolved into something like *Night of the Living Dead*. Fantasy and reality became one and the same.

CHAPTER 5

I Died, Just Not Permanently

"Out of college, money spent,
See no future, pay no rent.
All the money's gone, nowhere to go."
—John Lennon/Paul McCartney

Some people laugh at the mention of marijuana being a *gateway* drug, but for me it was. Since I had crossed one huge boundary— smoking pot after I swore alcohol was as far as I'd go—it seemed only natural to me that other drugs would follow suit. I was playing softball at Gladeville Park because getting high had finished whatever baseball career I might have had. On one particularly beautiful afternoon, I wasn't actually playing but had gone to the park just to hang out. That was when I took my first hit of speed, an Upjohn that had come from a Metro Nashville police lieutenant, which only increased my cynicism about the police. I washed it down with a Schlitz Malt Liquor.

Of course, as with every other drug I later encountered, I loved it. I had never felt anything like that chemically charged high, as if I could "leap over tall buildings in a single bound," like Superman. My senses were sharpened to a fine point, like a turbo-charged engine. I felt more alive. It was like waking up when you're already awake. That little pill opened the door to every other pill imaginable: uppers, downers, and all arounders. It did not matter what it was. I took it, and the more the better! If one was good, five were great!

That summer, after my first hit of speed, I discovered that I had a very high tolerance for drugs in general. This set up a sick pattern of taking so much of whatever I had that I would lose consciousness or simply pass out. Again, God's grace is the only reason I am still here to pass along my story. There were many times when I had no pulse or went into seizures. In other words, I died, just not permanently, as so many people I have known and loved did.

Rock and roll is in my DNA and has played a large part of who I am since the very beginning. I firmly believe the Beach Boys' Brian Wilson's sentiment: "Rock and roll is good for the soul." Rock and roll did not lead me down the path of addiction; it just made a great soundtrack! I'm sure music has always helped me form thought patterns and different ways of looking at things, from the natural beauty of God's hand in nature to the social fabric that somehow holds this frail planet together. Unfortunately, a large part of today's music, especially rap, sends a different, overt message of negativity, especially regarding women and drug use. Then again, I'm sure the generation prior to mine thought the same thing about my generation's music.

Amusingly, some people cannot figure out why I still attend rock and roll shows in my sixties. But to me, there is no magic superior to the butterflies in my stomach when the lights dim and out steps Mick Jagger singing "Jumping Jack Flash" or Bob Seger singing "Beautiful Loser/Traveling Man." I still cry every time I hear that song, especially live. I'm amazed that I've enjoyed the concerts where I've been straight during the last twenty years more than the ones where I was so wasted that, although I knew I was there, I really don't recall much. All I have are the ticket stubs or the T-shirts to prove to myself I was there.

My first concert was seeing Elvis Presley at Middle Tennessee State University (MTSU) in 1975. I had never seen anything like him before and never will again. From the first chord to the famous line "Elvis has left the building," I remember it all. Elvis may have left, but I was just entering my love affair with music and concerts.

In November 1975, I was back at that same venue to see the Who. I didn't know who they were before, but I would never forget them, as well as the other British rock bands. The Who concert was also the first time I had taken some purple haze acid. I had no idea what to expect, but that had never stopped me before. The Who were playing the rock opera *Tommy*, and I was tripping so much I thought Roger Daltrey was Jesus Christ as he emerged into the dazzling lights as Tommy reborn. With his long, curly hair and white outfit, he was the most beautiful, emotional, and charismatic thing this country boy had ever experienced. Although I don't suggest that anyone try acid, due to the different reactions people have, it does heighten the senses, to say the least.

All was well and good until we left the building. At first, we couldn't find the car, and when we finally did, I couldn't drive. We desperately wanted to get some alcohol to help us come down, but since they didn't sell beer after midnight back then, we just had to wait it out and come down naturally. I ended up lying down in a friend's apartment with my head against a speaker. I listened to Clark Rogers, a DJ on WKDF, *the* rock and roll station in Nashville. Rogers had the coolest, most laid-back voice on FM, the voice of the stoned, and I listened to him all night as I tried to get a grip on reality. Amazingly, he and I would cross paths years later in a healthier environment.

Thankfully, I had a strong mind because the only way to make it through a trip on hallucinogens is by keeping your cool and reminding yourself that what is not real is caused by the drug. The Who concert was the first of many, many acid trips. I loved it for partying and the loss of inhibitions it allowed me to feel. I also liked the way it expanded my mind, although I'm grateful that I didn't do too much irreparable damage to my brain with acid. Of course, one of the diabolical things about using drugs is that many times we don't realize the damage we have done until it is too late.

The summer following my high-school graduation in 1975, I was working at the Hermitage, which was President Andrew Jackson's home. My main task was to take care of Rachel's Garden, named after President Jackson's beloved wife. In addition, I maintained the tombs of Rachel and the president. I loved the job, and, while there, I developed my love of history. I learned that in 1806, future president Jackson killed a man who accused him of cheating on a horse race and then insulted Jackson's wife. Jackson shot the man in a duel. (Incidentally, in 1990, my construction company was fortunate enough to get the contract for restoring the Hermitage to its former glory.)

My first task every morning was to sweep and clean the tomb of the president and the first lady. This turned out to be a great place to smoke my first joint of the day to get things started off right. Not many people can say that they got to smoke a joint in a former president's tomb, much less every morning. I'm not bragging because, looking back, I realize it was disrespectful, but back then, it was pretty cool to me. One would also have to consider the context of the times. Everyone who worked there whom I knew got high in the seventies. The ones who didn't get high were the oddballs. Times really have changed, or have they? I am too old and "out of the loop" to really know.

My plans had been to attend East Tennessee State University in Johnson City, Tennessee, but along with my brain, those plans were altered. I don't remember exactly what happened in the process of applying, but by the end of August 1975, I was fortunate to be accepted into Volunteer State Community College. It is a fine institution in its own right but not a university, as I had planned on attending. I looked at it like it was merely an extension of high school and treated it as such. I found out that they also had standards, which I failed to meet. My life was all about getting high. As much as I enjoyed the college atmosphere, my number-one occupation was getting stoned: before, during, and after class. I had a deep interest in classes such as psychology and history, but when it came to a choice of either studying and applying myself academically or getting high, I don't have to tell you which option I chose.

CHAPTER 6

I'm Just Getting Started

"Because I'm eighteen, I get confused ev'ry day.
Eighteen, I just don't know what to say."
—Alice Cooper

Addiction is all about self-centeredness: me, me, and me. What can I do to make me happy? After all, I am the center of the universe. It sounds pitiful and childish, especially to me as I write this, but that is an addict's life. Naturally, my parents were watching me through all of this as my hair grew longer and my friends got rougher. I put as much distance between myself and my family and church as I could. One of my deepest regrets was when my grandmother (my father's mother) died. My Mamaw, whom I loved dearly, had passed away, and somehow I convinced my parents that I could not attend the funeral—the only truthful reason being that it would have interfered with my getting high. That was another checkmark in the guilt and shame column, which would grow considerably larger as the regrets piled up.

I was like a dog chasing its tail. When I got high, I did things that piled on guilt and shame. Because I was incapable of dealing with feelings, I had to use more drugs to bury those unwanted ones, which piled more guilt and shame on top of the ones I had just buried. I was caught in a quickly revolving downward spiral. It became painful to even look at myself in the mirror. Eventually, I could not bear for anyone else to look at me either for fear that they would see the monster I saw. Maybe I was not a monster, but I had become a pathetic excuse for a human being. Escape through drugs was the best answer I could come up with, but although they were killing me, they probably kept me from the final act of defeat: suicide. To quote a line from an NA pamphlet, which is part of the basic text, "Most of us realized that in our addiction we were slowly committing suicide, but addiction is such a cunning enemy of life that we had lost the power to do anything about it." That is where I was without knowing it and would remain for quite a while.

The winter of 1976 contains a lot of snapshots, but most of that period is blurry and out of focus to me. I was attempting to stay in college, working at the local Winn Dixie grocery store frying chicken, and doing lots of drugs. Wrecking cars became a way of life, and I'm sure my parents dreaded it when the phone rang, fearing that it would be the hospital or the police calling. My first wreck coincided with my first time taking Valium. I had taken five 10-milligram Valiums that afternoon and then proceeded to drive from West Nashville to Mount Juliet in rush-hour traffic, which is not an easy task even when straight. I made it with a friend in tow and went to a party, where I drank a lot of liquor and still drove around. I was in and out of a blackout all night.

I have no idea how I survived that night or how I made it through the night without being arrested. All I remember is winding up in a ditch about three hundred yards below my parents' house. I walked home, woke my father up, and asked him to get his tractor and pull me out of the ditch. There I was, stumbling down the road with a logging chain around my shoulders, to wait for my father. When he realized the shape I was in, he took the chain away and drove me back home. The car had to wait until the next morning to be towed in by Hamblen's Wrecker Service. We ended up being good customers of theirs. This was just one of many blatant examples of what I put myself and my parents through.

I was certainly traveling a long way from my Green Hill Church of Christ roots, where even dancing was frowned upon. My father had gone so far as to protest this sinful thing at a Wilson County Board of Education meeting. This attitude collided with me and my senior prom, where there would be a dance. My poor mother bribed me with a hundred dollars not to attend the dance. Of course, I bought a bunch of liquor with the money and made up for not attending the dance by getting hammered at the after-prom party. That is just an illustration of the irony and paradoxes of my life. I missed the sinful dance but made up for it by getting as drunk as possible afterward. It was not my mother's fault. As with most parents in that era, she thought she was doing the right thing by trusting me to do the right thing.

Many times when I share my story, people ask me why my parents didn't do something when they knew I was out of control. As I mentioned earlier, denial affects the family, as well as the addict. They were hoping it was just a phase I would grow out of, hopefully soon. However, it would be no time soon because I was just getting started.

Being raised with a long list of dos and don'ts, I got tired of the conflict. The "shalt nots" were much more fun. Of course, girls were in the "shalt not" column, but I was lustful before I even knew what the word meant. I always seemed to be in a state of conflict. The rules of right and wrong, which I was raised not only to believe but to obey, left me with feelings of turmoil. I came to realize later that the struggle was in my spirit, not in my religion.

My life was wrapped around an ever-increasing amount of drugs: Quaaludes, Valium, speed, crystal T, cocaine, and acid, with a lot of alcohol thrown in for good measure. Beer was never my thing, though I drank plenty of it. In those days, there were no liquor stores in Wilson County, so we had to rely on bootleggers to supply us with cheap whiskey. I almost never took drugs without mixing them with alcohol, a deadly combination that resulted in trips to jail and car accidents.

My first encounter with jail happened when I was charged with public intoxication for urinating on West Main Street in Lebanon. My feeling of helplessness was overwhelming, as I was handcuffed and thrown in the back of a police car. Thankfully, I was able to get out on bond quickly, although I was later arrested several more times. My lawyer gave me some good advice, which I have never forgotten: never plead guilty under any circumstances. His point was that once you pled guilty, there was no room for leverage. I received probation, and it was quickly forgotten. It's funny how you are scared to death on the way to jail, but once you are out, it doesn't seem like such a big deal. The wake-up calls go unheeded.

Because I wasn't successful in college, I worked odd jobs and dealt some drugs to supply my own voracious appetite for destruction. I had no particular preference for any particular drug at that time; anything would do and lots of it. However, one of my favorites was crystal T, which I shared with my favorite running buddy, Steve. It was a very strange drug. Most people tried it once and swore off it like it was poison, which it was. Sometimes it made me euphoric; at other times, I would hallucinate; and still other times I would be mentally paralyzed and could not even speak.

Originally, this strange drug came in wafers but was later converted into a crystalline powder that could be snorted or shot. Some people said it was horse tranquilizer made in laboratories by God knows who. I don't really know. What I do know is that it took me to some strange places. In the late 1970s, I was informed that I had some brain damage by neurosurgeons who were diagnosing my migraine headaches. This made sense because I experienced many days in a row when I was incoherent in thought and speech and felt numbness in my head. I was literally a numbskull. I just hoped it would go away. Meanwhile, I was doing more and more drugs, and I even felt perverse pride in being able to do more than the people around me and keep going when they could not. Although this was very sick thinking, it was indicative of where I was at the time. Only God's grace kept me from going over the edge permanently.

By 1976, I was running with a bunch of guys and girls who were really into the drug scene. They had been at it for a while, but I was still a relative rookie. I must admit that there was a dark attraction to hanging with people who were so far away from my upbringing. I was even running with some of the guys who had wanted to kill me for being a supposed narc back in school.

One fateful day started like any other: getting up and searching for drugs with whoever knew where to get them. Drinking was my foundation at the time, and my partner and I were drinking and taking some Placidyls, a strong sedative that had the nickname "greenie meanies." Between them and the alcohol, I was wasted by the middle of the day. Though I don't remember why, we ended up at a girl's apartment. I was very high and sat in the living room while people were milling about. Since I was the new kid on the block, I minded my own business.

At some point, someone led me to a bedroom where three or four people were in a walk-in closet, cooking up what I soon discovered was heroin. This was my first time seeing heroin or anyone shooting up, for that matter. My friend Keith asked if I wanted a shot, and just as naturally as if I had been doing it all my life, I stuck my arm out and got off. Man, did I get off! It was nothing like I had previously experienced. I was warm and euphoric, not understanding that I had just crossed over to the dark side. I felt the bomb explode that I had been waiting for since my first drink of alcohol. I had lit the fuse early on, but this was the day it went off. I was in love.

I went back to the living room and luxuriated in that warm feeling of not having a care in the world. My entire life up until then had been spent worrying about being good enough. However, that day I finally felt like I fit in, only in the wrong place. Everyone else was nodding out, as heroin junkies do, but not me. I loved that feeling so much that I didn't want it to end, and I wanted more. One shot and I was off to the races. Later, we went and got some more from a dealer who eventually crashed in one of the worst wrecks I would ever be in. In it, he lost his life.

When it was all over, I was disgusted with myself, full of self-loathing. Although I had no idea where it was all heading, I did know that I couldn't change what I had done, which scarred me deep inside. I had just crossed a line bigger than any previous one: I had shot up, that thing reserved for junkies, the thing that was the worst taboo and simply was not done where I came from. If you had told me when I was a kid that I would either go to Mars or be a junkie, I would have packed my bags for Mars. There was absolutely no way that this good old Church of Christ country boy would ever stick a needle in his arm. But I did, and it left me with a dark stain on my soul that I have been trying to erase ever since. I had unleashed a monster that would kick my butt for many years.

As much as I liked my initiation into shooting heroin, I didn't do it the next day or the next. What I had done was similar to losing one's virginity. I rationalized that because I had done it once, I might as well keep going. What was there to lose? A lot, actually, and if I had left it at that, things might have gone much differently. For a while, I kept away. I remember the dirty feeling I got while working at the Winn Dixie the next night. I knew I had gone totally against society's norms. Being called a junkie was worse than being called a prostitute. I was becoming what I had always shunned. I was like a leper, on the fringe of society and no longer a part of it. Above all, I wanted to keep it hidden from my other partying friends.

People often ask me why I continued to do something when it brought on such bad feelings afterward. My best answer goes back to the sexual analogy. How many people have had sex one time, felt guilty about it, and then quit? The answer is not many, if any. The rush I got from heroin and later Dilaudid was instantaneous. It was like a chemically induced orgasm. Knowing I was only a heartbeat away from that dreamlike rush of opiates was very appealing. Add that to the fact that I was already an addict, and it was the perfect storm. I used to scream at my father, "Let me shoot up Ronald Reagan with narcotics, and he would get hooked!" My point was that anyone is subject to addiction once he or she starts abusing narcotics. One out of ten are the odds. Not everyone does become an addict, but the odds are very high that a person will. The next ten years of my life I lived like an animal, chasing that magic feeling I found in that closet on my first day. Whatever morals or ethics I had were traded for my next high. I was a junkie.

That started ten years of utter insanity, as I tried to run from what I did by doing more of what I had done to feel the way I did in the first place. I ran hard and fast from myself, but, as the old saying goes, "Wherever you go, there you are." Perhaps the reason a junkie resembles an animal over time is that an addict is reduced to the primal state of survival, and to an addict, survival means pleasure at any cost. The old werewolf movies used to show a man slowly turning into a beast. That is the same thing a junkie does, only slower. Finally, the day comes when junkies can't bear to look at themselves in the mirror, and they wonder why they don't slash their jugular while shaving—that is, if they are still bathing or shaving at that point. Before my introduction to the needle, I had tried filling that hole in my soul with anything I could get. After the needle, that hole became a bottomless pit that was impossible to fill, though I did my best.

My father had gotten me a job with the Teamsters Union in 1976. I was considered a "casual worker," which meant I worked through whichever freight company needed me—for example, Yellow Freight. It was a great job for a nineteen-year-old kid, but it did not interfere with my drug use. In fact, the good pay only made matters worse because I had more money to get high on.

While working there, I was doing a lot of speed and cocaine, both snorting and IV. I stayed up two or three days in a row while trying to work. It was hard, back-breaking work, loading trucks on the docks. It must have been winter because I remember wearing many layers of clothes. I was working away one day, and the next thing I remember was waking up in the heated break room, lying on the floor with a bunch of people looking down at me. An ambulance arrived and took me to the ER, where they informed me that I had experienced a grand mal seizure.

Thankfully, that was before the days of drug testing, so that issue never came up.

Since I had a cousin who was an epileptic, it was ascertained that I was one as well. Although I knew that speed and cocaine, coupled with sleep deprivation and hard labor, had caused the seizure, I chose to be labeled an epileptic, rather than a drug addict. They prescribed me Dilantin to keep the seizures at bay. To my way of thinking, all I had to do was take the pills; then I could continue with cocaine and speed without the trouble of having seizures. I even went so far as to wear one of those emergency tags around my neck for years.

I was way out there in my rationalizations, and I had just begun tearing myself down physically, mentally, and emotionally. But much more was to follow. The human body is truly an amazing creation, when you think about it. The body can take an unbelievable amount of abuse and keep functioning and, somehow, miraculously regenerate. We are marvelously made, though I am sure God did not intend for addicts to punish our bodies as we do.

We spent summers or anytime the weather was warm enough at either Cedar Creek or Langford's Cove on Old Hickory Lake, a man-made lake that stretched over nine counties in Middle Tennessee. We drank a lot of beer and passed joints around, as well as whatever else was available. Yet even in the midst of this hardcore partying, something positive resulted for me. The guys were always daring one another to do something, and on one particular day it was to go jogging. We were drinking Miller Longnecks, which was a step up from what we usually drank. For whatever reason, a few of us took off running. We didn't cover very much ground because we were drunk and stumbling, but something special happened to me as I ran in those old Converse sneakers: I became a runner. That was in 1976, and since then I have run more than 15,000 miles, plus a marathon.

That was the first time I had run around a track without a coach forcing me to do it, and I liked it. Running fit in well with my rebellious nature. Running was something I did by myself and for myself. Whatever the reason, running was something I would stick with for many years. It was also an addiction, but it was a positive one. It was one thing that I actually started and continued.

I even got to a point where I would buy my Dilaudid in the James Casey Homes and then go to nearby Shelby Park, where I ran for two miles before shooting up my pills. I figured I would get a better high after the natural endorphins from running kicked in. It is similar to a bulimic who eats and then vomits afterward. I had some kind of crazy counterbalance thing going on where I would justify the negativity of shooting dope with the positive energy produced by running. I have to say that running got me over withdrawals quicker when I chose to get clean, and the positive effects of running helped my body cope with the abuse I gave it.

I was fortunate to get hired on full time at the Ford Glass plant in 1977. I'm sure my father thought this would give me stability and a future because I didn't seem to have one of my own. That was when I at least tried to work, before I gave up the pretense of even trying. I was placed in the same department as my father, except he worked the day shift as an inspector, and I worked nights. I know I became an embarrassment to him when he came in at 8:00 a.m. to relieve me. He wouldn't know whether I had made it in or not until he checked in and, if I was there, what shape I was in. The golden boy he used to brag about had become a long-haired, red-eyed monster. I had been handed a great opportunity, and it was not one that a person should squander, though, of course, I eventually did.

My father and I came from two totally different generations, mine being the spoiled, self-centered one. I wanted what I wanted when I wanted it, without giving much thought to whom it affected.

Working at Ford in the late seventies was great for kids my age. Hundreds of us, mostly straight out of high school, would meet up at the credit union on Friday mornings. It was like a carnival with the parking lot full of people with drugs for sale, not to mention plenty of hot, cheap merchandise. Some of the guys made more on payday than they did for a whole week's wages at the plant. Coincidentally, the Tennessee State Prison is located right across the Cumberland River, and many of those guys went straight from working for Ford to working for the state. Thankfully, I was not among them.

While most of my friends had gone on to college, had families, and started careers, I dived deeper into using drugs around the clock. If it hadn't been for the union, I would have been fired long before I actually was. I didn't mind working, as long as it didn't interfere with my drug use.

CHAPTER 7

The Storm Rages

"Whiskey bottles and brand new cars,
Oak tree you're in my way."
—Lynyrd Skynyrd

In 1977, I totaled out three cars in six months but survived. Sometimes at work, the glass furnaces would shut down, and some people were lucky enough to get sent home with pay. One night I was chosen to go home, which was great, but I had ridden to work with my friend Mike. He drove a 1976 Ford 4-wheel drive F-150 pickup truck. He loved that truck and kept it immaculate. For some reason he let me drive it to go shoot pool with some other guys until it was time to pick him up. That might have worked had I not been taking Valium, drinking, and smoking pot. The next thing I remembered was waking up in the Neurological Intensive Care Unit with a lot of other seriously ill folks.

I was told that I had left a friend's house close to the plant but somehow ended up in downtown Nashville. The traffic lights continued to blink until 6:00 a.m., and shortly before that time, I had run through a traffic light and was t-boned by a Mack dump truck. If I hadn't been sitting up so high, I would have been crushed underneath the dump truck. However, it was bad enough. The grill of the truck came through my window, broke my skull in two places, and embedded pieces of glass in my head, which took years to work their way out.

I ended up at what used to be Baptist Hospital until it was taken over by St Thomas, but poor Mike's truck was totaled. He came out after the night shift was over, but neither his truck nor I was anywhere to be found. He started a frantic search for me and the truck. This was before computers came on the scene, and information was not readily available to the police, who had an APB out on me. My whereabouts could not be disclosed because I was an adult, and by law the hospital had to protect my privacy. Because I had not given permission, no one was notified. My father had some choice words for Baptist Hospital for keeping everyone in the dark for thirty-six hours until I woke up and told the hospital to call my parents. My poor mother and father had scoured the neighborhood and my old haunts, desperately searching for me or anyone who might have known where I was. They were terrified with not knowing and assuming the worst. Unfortunately, that was just the beginning of those late-night calls that every parent dreads.

Meanwhile, Mike didn't know where his beloved truck was, while the doctors were busy wiring my skull back together. They had to go through my temple and the side of my nose to do it. It left some scars that are still visible today. Miraculously, there was no brain damage. God had seen me through this accident and several more brushes with possible death, paralysis, or living in a vegetative state.

Any fool would have taken that wreck as a wake-up call, but not me. It didn't even register how fortunate I was to be alive. I simply dealt with it as I did everything else: I got higher and higher. Eventually, there would be repercussions such as DUIs and losing my license, but I even skated through those relatively easily. If I had been a cat, I would have been on the second of my nine lives with the intention of using them all.

About two months after that catastrophe, I went out with a bunch of guys from work to a friend's boat on the lake and partied. I had worked all night and had been getting high at work. As soon as I left work, and certainly when we got to the lake, we followed marijuana and beer with Valium and Quaaludes. Anyway, I'd promised to give a guy a ride back toward work. I had no business driving, especially through downtown Nashville in the middle of the day, but I did.

As I got close to downtown, I must have forgotten that I was driving because even though I was in the slow lane, I ran over a pest control truck with bright bugs painted all over it. My 1965 Ford Fairlane, which I had driven only a few weeks, was totaled. Thank God, neither the passenger nor I was injured. When I came to my senses, I was talking to a Metro police officer and the pest control guy. The guy was not hurt either, just mad. I tried to walk and talk but couldn't, so I was taken downtown, presumably to be arrested for DUI and causing the wreck. By the time we reached the station, though, I was able to pass a field sobriety test. Funny what you can do when you set your mind to it. All the way down, I had been pleading ignorance. Plus, I had my epileptic tag around my neck, which came in handy. So the officer came around to my side, with me helping him along. The result was three more points against my license, plus the loss of another car, but I walked away. It was another wake-up call that I refused to acknowledge.

My final wreck in that bizarre six-month trilogy began with

my purchase of a 1969 Pontiac GTO equipped with a Ram-400 engine and a four-speed transmission. I had dreamed of owning a GTO ever since I was a kid. A guy in Mount Juliet had one and used to drag race it on the street. To me, it was the ultimate hot rod. That car used to cruise comfortably at 110 to 120 miles per hour, even loaded down with people. I raced a Corvette one night with six people in my GTO, one of them a girl who sat in the middle on the console. I was a dangerous but good driver if I wasn't too high.

My third wreck happened one night when I was hanging out with a guy who was one of the first junkies I had ever met as a kid. We never ran around together, but on that particular night we did. I had a date with a friend of his wife's. She and I were drinking and taking Valium early that evening and decided to go to his house. The only thing I remember clearly (Valium is very hard on the memory) was being at a Texaco station and the guy pouring more Valium in my hand, which I promptly swallowed. My next memory is of getting out of bed beside the girl I was with and thinking I had to get home. I looked around and realized it was a stupid idea. I was in a nice, safe place, and there was a thunderstorm brewing outside, not to mention that I was too high to drive. Nevertheless, I was a homeboy, and back then, home was with Mom and Dad.

My route was up Scotts Hollow Hill, where I had topped out at more than 120 miles per hour the previous Saturday night, though I was going in the opposite direction down the hill then. However, this time the circumstances were different. I was in a Valium-and-liquor blackout. I was told later that I was doing about 80 miles per hour. I passed a subdivision on my left and lost control of my car. The car corkscrewed through a telephone pole and landed right-side up. This was before airbags, when everyone rode without seatbelts, and I ended up in the back seat with my feet sticking out the rear windshield. Fortunately, the only serious injury I sustained was a bunch of glass in my butt. Some friends of mine, who were coming home from a date, said they knew it was me by the orange Converse tennis shoes that were my trademark.

I woke up in the Donelson Hospital emergency room, only to see a state trooper standing next to my father. I immediately passed back out. The state trooper had a blood test run on me, and I was charged with DUI. The next time I woke up, I was in Vanderbilt's ICU, along with other men in vegetative states. The doctors were not sure whether I had sustained any brain damage, due to the violence of the accident and the fact that I had not regained consciousness. I wasn't there long because the only damage they found was the glass in my butt. The result: more points against my license (which were adding up fast), a DUI, and an $1,800 bill from Nashville Electric Service for having to come out on a stormy night and restore power to the subdivision I had flown past. Needless to say, 1977 was not one of my better years.

CHAPTER 8

Nothing Is Going to Slow Me Down

"Once you're gone, you can't come back,
When you're out of the blue and into the black."
—Neil Young

In 1979, I was doing my usual thing, snorting crystal T and hanging out with anyone who wanted to party. I had a group of girls, totally platonic, called "George's Angels." They were three younger girls who used to hang out with me, drinking beer and doing whatever else came along. We were watching softball at a park and decided to get some beer. I had some THC in the car, but I left it and the three pretty girls when I ran into an old buddy, Bob Eskew. Talk about not having your priorities in order. He said he could get some Dilaudid in Lebanon, so off I went, assuring the angels I would meet them later.

Although Bob lived in Lebanon and knew of all the places to buy drugs, it was one of those days when you had money but couldn't find any. Other times, when you were broke, everyone you knew could get something. That was just a junkie's life. Finally, we decided to give up and go back to my car where the THC was. Bob was not too keen on T, but to a needle junkie, any drug is better than no drug. It's what is known as a "needle jones."

We were in a hurry to get to the dope. We crossed I-40 on highway 231 south. Bob had that old Lincoln Town Car rolling, and I saw the needle hit 90 miles per hour. We were covering some ground. Dusk was beginning to fall. Suddenly, I felt a jolt in the right rear of the car from what I believed was a blown tire. Bob was fighting the steering wheel as we crossed over into the oncoming traffic side of the highway. We were going sideways, and thank God, no one was coming. I was later told that the cars coming from the other direction had seen what was happening and had the good sense to stop. All I remember is gripping the dash to keep from sliding out of the car, as we skidded from side to side.

My side of the car hit the opposite side of a bridge, and I flew out of the passenger window down into a creek bed about ninety feet below. Poor Bob stayed in the car and ricocheted back across the bridge to the opposite side, then careened back to my side and broke through a concrete wall, landing about forty feet from where I lay. When I awoke, people were attempting to help me up, but whenever they tried, my leg gave out as if it were asleep. I had broken my pelvis and my nose. I looked over to see people trying to help Bob out of the car.

Somehow, I made my way to the ambulance, but the attention seemed to be focused on Bob. As I saw him on the gurney, I knew why. His head had swollen to the size of a basketball and had turned a sickening shade of purple. They asked me to exit the ambulance in order to get him in. I'm sure I was in shock. I was asked to sit in the passenger seat of the ambulance with my pelvis broken, as I tried to staunch the flow of blood from my nose. Bob was immediately rushed into the E.R., while I sat in a chair and waited.

I don't remember how long it was, but a state trooper came out with a serious look on his face and told me Bob didn't make it. I mumbled, "I was afraid of that." They discovered my broken pelvis, but luckily it was broken in a way that would not require surgery. I stayed in the hospital for a week and on crutches for a few weeks more, which would have slowed most people down but not me. I charged right back into my wild life. I never looked back long enough to realize another human being, who had been sitting right beside me, had lost his life, and how blessed I was to be alive. To me, it was just another bump in the road: I was lucky, he wasn't, and all the lies you tell yourself when you don't want to face reality. I was insane, and I am still haunted today over Bob's death. He had children who lost their father. I had scared my parents to death yet again. All this time God was showing me how full of grace and mercy He is, but I refused to listen.

CHAPTER 9

Running Wide Open and Out of Control

"Can't you hear me knockin' on your window?"
—Mick Jagger/Keith Richards

My father had told me that if a man was not willing to work, he would beg, borrow, or steal. As I increased my drug usage, I became more willing to steal. I was working, but by 1978, it wasn't enough to support my growing drug habit. I stole to get money for drugs and then ended up in after-hours places to get them. There was a sick thrill in being someplace I wasn't supposed to be and getting away with it, like hearing alarms and knowing the police were on their way. Of course, I was afraid, but I didn't really take the time to fully comprehend that what I was doing could send me to prison or get me killed.

Our reputation with the police was so bad that one night we were pulled over by a Wilson County Sheriff's patrol officer, and even though he found an open bottle of Crown Royal, and we were totally wasted, he let us go. He was looking for hot merchandise, which we were guilty of stealing, but he was disappointed when he didn't find any. Naturally, he confiscated our Crown Royal, while complimenting us on our good taste in whiskey.

One cold night in the winter of 1978, we pushed our luck by breaking into an orthodontist's office we had already hit once. We came out with a good cache of narcotics. That particular night it was my turn to go through the window, my partner being the driver. Usually, he did the dirty work, but that night it fell to me. I broke the window with a hammer after many tries, but, unbeknownst to me, a silent alarm was triggered as I broke the glass. I should have known something was wrong because the window and everything were different. There was nothing worth having when I got in, and when I crawled through the window to get out, I heard the awful sound of sirens fast approaching. I made it to a concrete culvert, but I was too late. The police had brought a K-9 unit with them, and I was quickly apprehended.

The sound of a snarling German shepherd is a frightening thing. I lay as still as I could to keep the dog from shredding me, while two Metro Police officers had shotguns aimed at me from either side. I was grabbed up, thrown down, and searched. Then they asked where my partner was. I played dumb and said I was alone. That made them angrier, but I knew that if you get caught, you go down alone, you don't narc—that street mentality! They threw me into a car and whisked me off downtown to be booked and jailed. I had heard horror stories about the old jail, where the elevator would stop and prisoners were beaten. I figured I was a prime candidate because I refused to be a snitch. I was charged with third-degree burglary and was given a $5,000 bond. I made the most dreaded call of my life to the only person who could help me: my father. He came right down and, being the good father he was, signed a property bond so I could be released. I'm sure he was angry, but he was also a compassionate man who couldn't bear to think of his son sitting in that nasty Nashville jail. I cannot imagine the nightmare my parents had to endure back then. Thank God, they lived to see me make it to the other side, but that would be a ways off.

I was in shock. All of the other times when I had done those crazy things, I had gotten away with it, but this time I got caught, and it was time to pay the piper. So, the next day my father and I went to the apartment of my friend and partner in crime to gather my few belongings because I was moving back home. He probably thought my father was out for blood because my father knew we'd been together the previous night and many nights before that. Instead, my father simply told him that maybe we could be around each other someday but not then. Those words will always be special to me because after many years of being apart, I got a call from my friend, asking for help in recovery. God is good.

I had to get a lawyer to see what I was actually facing. Luckily, my record was fairly clean. I learned a valuable lesson on that first visit: find a lawyer who knows how to work the system, a fixer. Unfortunately, that lawyer did not fit the bill. He was a good lawyer in other areas, but criminal law was not his forte. I got nervous when he had to pull a law book off the shelf to see exactly what the law had to say about third-degree burglary and what the standard sentence was. However, my father had faith in him, and because my father was my bondsman, I really had no choice but to play along.

Back then, there were alcoholic treatment centers but not much in the way of drug treatment. The good men of the Employee Assistance Program at Ford tried to get me to go to AA meetings, but to no avail. Although I drank every day, I was not an alcoholic.

I just liked to drink. Somehow, it was arranged that I go to Parthenon Pavilion, a psychiatric hospital. The plan was for me to get help but, more important, to look good for the judge. I still had not considered that I was an addict. Alcoholism had gained some social acceptance, but to be a drug addict was to be a pariah.

When I entered Parthenon, I had no idea what to expect. Mostly, I remember jogging around the gym to keep my sanity and reading Ken Kesey's *One Flew Over the Cuckoo's Nest*. The movie had just come out, and with my sick sense of humor, I thought I was like Mac in the movie, who goes to the insane asylum to beat going to prison but gets beat by the system in the end. I remember playing Ping-Pong with an older lady who was heavily medicated (doing the Thorazine shuffle). Since she was in slow motion, I had to play in slow motion, and it somehow struck me as bizarre.

The court date arrived quickly. I pleaded guilty, rather than try and fight it. Terms had been prearranged, but nothing was final until the judge signed off, and I had a tough one. Judge A. A. Birch, the first black judge in Nashville, had an imposing, no-nonsense manner. The new courthouse in Nashville was named after him. He was not one to utter idle threats; he meant what he said. I was one scared little white boy. You understand the true meaning of powerlessness when one man can decide whether you get to go home or live in a small concrete box.

I was sentenced to eleven months and twenty-nine days. The sentence was suspended on condition of five years' supervised probation, including regular drug tests. At first, I had weekly meetings with my probation officer, and then my drug testing was transferred to my doctor at Parthenon. The doctor was an arrogant little man, and he decided that I should have blood tests, instead of urine samples. He was as invasive in my life as he could be, as if I were his pet. Of course, I was powerless, so I had to either do as he said or go to jail. To give an example of his attitude toward me, he told me I should take up karate. I thought that was good, positive advice to help me change my lifestyle, but he quickly followed it up by saying it would come in handy in jail because that's where I was going.

I stayed under his iron hand for a few months until I was finally able to beg my way out. He allowed me to go to Dede Wallace Center for counseling and drug tests, which were urine tests. It eventually came out that while I was under his care, he was going to the YMCA and taking care of other men in the restroom stalls. He was busted for his little escapades but eventually redeemed himself by starting Sex Anonymous meetings in Nashville. It couldn't have happened to a nicer guy. As they say, "What goes around comes around."

Dede Wallace was the first place where I had ever been counseled about my drug abuse, and they tried to help me. My first counselor was a man named James, who was able to make me see that the only answers of any value would have to come from within me. Although I grew up with answers from well-intentioned people, they obviously did not work, as I was seemingly incapable of doing "like I should." It was time for me to be an adult, to think like an adult, and to stop depending on others for my answers. That was difficult because I was all scrambled up inside, but it started my long, positive journey toward recovery and redemption.

I stayed away from illegal drugs for some time but continued to drink. I still could not accept that I had a problem with alcohol, and it was legal. I remember leaving Parthenon, overcome with a sense of freedom. I had an epiphany (or so I thought) that as long as I did not stick a needle in my arm, I would be all right. I knew that

I had to chill with other illegal drugs, but the arm dope was the real culprit. It certainly couldn't be that my life was out of control. I still didn't see that I was powerless over my addiction and that my life was unmanageable.

I stayed on probation for a couple more years, with the drug tests being dropped toward the end. My father asked the UAW to go back in front of Judge Birch for me, which they did, to ask that I be released from probation because I was rehabilitated and had seen the error of my ways. The UAW representative went with me into the judge's chambers to sign the release forms, and then the judge said that he would like to speak with me in private. He clearly let me know that he was doing it as a favor to the UAW and my family, not because he really believed in me. I suppose he had a lot of experience with addicts, who are not the most reliable people. He did tell me that if I ever appeared before him again, I should pack my toothbrush because I would be going to the penitentiary. Thank God that even though I didn't stay straight, I never had to go in front of him again.

CHAPTER 10

I Won't Get Out of This World Alive

"Sleep all day, out all night,I know what you're doin'."
—The James Gang

I was laid off from Ford for the last time in April 1980. Those three years consisted of car wrecks, getting into big trouble, and learning how to be a proficient drug addict. A lot of dealing and other shady activities filled in the gaps. That is why many guys from Ford made that short leap across the Cumberland River to Tennessee State Prison. So, with a year's pay at 95 percent, I had a lot of time on my hands.

I became involved with a young lady, and we moved in together. It was probably not a healthy situation for her because anyone who had anything to do with me was volunteering for trouble. My lifestyle was very apparent. We spent eighteen months partying and even talked about marriage. I proposed and gave her a half-carat diamond ring. Actually, it wasn't a real diamond; it was zirconium, but what she didn't know wouldn't hurt her. Oh, well, it worked, and I saved some money. I was not very honest, and she left me before we made the mistake of marrying. I eventually made amends to her. One of the few bright spots in my heavy addiction years was that I did not get married and/or have kids. That would have been a nightmare, especially for the children. It was just another example of God doing for me what I could not do for myself. I had hurt enough people without adding children to the list.

The TV show *Dallas* debuted in 1978, and the movie *Urban Cowboy* came out in 1980. Suddenly, everyone was a cowboy or a cowgirl. Nightclubs had sprung up all over the country with the *Urban Cowboy* theme, complete with two-step line dancing and mechanical bulls, like in Gilley's bar in Fort Worth, Texas. Blazing Saddles, one of those clubs, opened in Nashville, and my soon-to-be ex-girlfriend and some friends and I became regulars. We were there every Friday and Saturday night, drinking, doing drugs like THC, and dancing. My father had been a good dancer, and I suppose I inherited his dancing genes. I enjoyed dancing, and it was a good way to meet women. Obviously, it was a good way for women to meet men as well because Betty met a guy there and left me high and dry. Although it bummed me out then, I am grateful now.

I became friendly with some of the doormen and the bouncers there, and they offered me a job working the mechanical bull. I also had to stock the bar and do other things before 7:00 p.m., but then it was show time. It was as close to entertaining as I had gotten. I met pretty girls who wanted to ride, as well as the rodeo cowboys who wanted the fastest and hardest ride I could give them. I also had fun throwing off the loud, obnoxious ones. The bull could be set at speeds from one through ten, and our bull, which came from Gilley's, had an extra gear. I would crank it to the maximum if I knew the rider wouldn't get hurt. But there were mattresses all over, so the biggest thing to get hurt was their pride.

I worked until 3:00 a.m. and drank during the last three or

four hours of every shift. It was a dream job for an addict, though it was also a positive experience. After we closed, we would either go home with someone we shouldn't have or continue partying. Either one was okay. The thing about working in a nightclub is that there's always trouble around the next corner. That was also where I met my good friend Greg. He was a Vietnam veteran who worked the door, drove a new Corvette, and was heavy into weightlifting. We ran around on most summer days in his Corvette and spent time on the water in his jet boat. Greg was also good looking, reminding me of Burt Reynolds from his *Smoky and the Bandit* days, so he was a chick magnet. He had been around and knew how to take care of himself.

He also kept a 9-millimeter pistol holstered when he worked the door, so I felt safe. He was another of those slightly older guys I gravitated toward, and I learned a lot about how to act out in the world. He helped me with weightlifting, and I helped him with running. He was not a junkie, which made him a good influence on me. We smoked a lot of pot, and I drank. I stayed fairly straight for close to a year, working at the club and chasing women. That was as close as I got to being a functioning addict. Somehow, I didn't shoot up for almost a year and was in the best shape I had ever been in. It turned out to be just a time-out, though, because soon I was running wide open again.

Between the end of 1981 and the beginning of 1982, two different events propelled me back into my old lifestyle. The first was when I went to the Smoky Mountains and stayed in a chalet with some friends, all couples, except for me. I had not taken any acid in over a year, but someone brought some, and I decided to take a hit. Of course, I was the life of the party, walking on beams twenty-five feet above the floor and along railings on the deck, which was suspended over the mountains. I was normally afraid of heights, but alcohol and acid always pushed me to do things that weren't normal for me. In a way, doing drugs is thrill seeking, like mountain climbing or sky diving. It's all about the rush.

When I got home, I did what I had always done; I started taking more and more acid, which went on for about six months. I took it as if it were speed, while going to nightclubs and drinking. On New Year's Eve, I ended up taking ten hits of blotter acid, which had a picture of Snoopy on them. I don't know how I was able to maintain, but I did. With some drugs, there is a peak point at which, no matter how many you take, the high only hits a certain level—but it was very high that night.

Shortly afterward, I ran into two of my old dope-shooting buddies, got some Dilaudid, and started shooting dope like I never had before. My addiction had waited patiently, while I was being relatively good. That animal lust for the narcotic rush flooded me. No matter how well I had been functioning, the current episode of my life was about to end abruptly.

Then began the dead years, as I refer to them, because they were all about dope and degradation. I had not yet found the hope I would later find in recovery. I came to believe that I was doomed. Even my mother was resigned to the fact that I would probably die from using drugs. I thought that every day for the rest of my life would be consumed with doing whatever it took to get more dope. Thankfully, God had other plans. During that time in the wilderness, I met the woman whom I fell hopelessly in love with, and I am more in love with her today than on the day I met her!

Once I'd started, the devil was easily able to snare me. Though I have never been a slave in the physical sense, I certainly have been a slave to drugs and everything that goes along with them, and I obeyed my masters faithfully. I was trapped in mind and body and thought my only means of escape would be to take more poison. I became willing to do anything, even sell my soul for a moment of relief, though in return for that brief period of relief, I only tightened my own chains further.

Suicide became a real and sometimes appealing alternative, and I began to understand what drives people to take that drastic measure. I have known quite a few people who committed suicide because of addiction. At one time I couldn't understand, but eventually I could relate to their feelings of desperation. I knew the feelings of helplessness and despair, a dark awareness that there was no way out but using until I died, and thinking, *Why not check out? I'm already in a dark, hopeless place.* But somehow, God gave me enough hope to keep on going until I was ready to change.

CHAPTER 11

The Modern-Day Prodigal Son

"You gotta learn to crawl before you learn to walk,
but I just couldn't listen to all that righteous talk"
—Aerosmith

A pivotal year for me was 1983. I attended my first 12-step meeting,
entered my first treatment center, and began a relationship with
the woman who owns my heart. My mother, who was also my
chief enabler, found a phone number in a newspaper article
about a group of people who met to help drug addicts: Narcotics
Anonymous. I already wanted help by then. Although I didn't
really want to stop using, I knew I couldn't last much longer. My
mother asked whether I would meet with a guy she had talked on
the phone with. I mainly told her yes to satisfy her and keep the
pipeline of enabling open. I had no idea what would happen or
what I expected, but that night changed my life forever. The fellow
who greeted me at the door of the meeting place was a guy I had
known from Ford. He used to sell me drugs and use Dilaudid, just
like me. He told me that he had been clean for over a year. That
seemed like an eternity to me because I couldn't go twelve hours
without being sick. Dilaudid withdrawals are horribly painful and

come on very fast. This was the first of a series of "coincidences" that began happening in my life as I started my rocky road to recovery. I know now that those coincidences were inspired by God and not merely happenstance. I was so sick that I wasn't even aware I was asking for help, but I knew the prayers of righteous people were being sent on my behalf. While I lay with the swine, people far off were praying for this prodigal son to return home.

Although I did not miraculously stay clean after that first meeting, a switch had turned on in my heart. No matter how far away I wandered, I knew my only hope was in those church basement rooms, along with the other addicts who sought relief from the despair and hopelessness of addiction. Things got much worse before they got better, but a seed had been planted. Those people actually understood me. Around them, I did not feel like an alien from another planet. I knew that when I was ready, I could throw up my hands and say, "I've had enough." When that finally happened a few years later, I knew I had a chance for the first time since I had stuck a needle in my arm.

I somehow obtained my real estate license in 1983. I had a hard time staying in class for having to shoot up, but I made it. I passed the test on my second try, and then I was on my way. To all outward appearances, I should have been a success, but being a junkie is not conducive to success. I worked in an office, but having to make frequent trips to Nashville to get drugs made things rather uncomfortable. My arms and hands were always swollen and bruised, and I had to come up with some excuse every day to explain it. The poor people around me had no idea they were working with a raving lunatic.

In July of that year, I made an attempt to get clean and got into Cumberland Heights Treatment Center. The lady who was the secretary in our office had become very close to me, and she took me there and dropped me off. Karen was a good Christian woman who had no idea what an addict was, but instead of judging, she just helped. She became like my second mother. I wish more of us Christians were like that humble lady.

I had no idea what I was getting into. I had tried some outpatient counseling before, but it didn't take. I was physically addicted and needed to be detoxed, as well as receive long-term help. It is amazing how withdrawals can erase the desire to get clean, but anyway, there I was. After detox, I moved in with some other guys who were there for the same reason. Among those guys was one of my all-time favorite guitarists, whom I had been a huge fan of. I saw him hitting some golf balls and thought he was a biker I used to buy drugs from who also had tattoos on his arms. We were in the same cabin, and he even played some tunes for us on an acoustic guitar. This showed me that no matter whether you are a rock legend or a country boy like me, addiction will rob you of everything, as it had him.

It was great meeting a rock star and all, but after thirty-six hours, I was on the road with my younger brother. I was so sick that I was smoking homegrown pot just to try to feel better. Denial is a powerful thing, and I had it bad. The middle of the dead years was in full bloom.

The last but most important event that changed my life occurred on my birthday, September 30, 1983. I had turned twenty-five years old, and some friends and I had a birthday party. I am notorious for arranging my own birthday parties—another control issue, I suppose. It was a warm night, so the party was held outside as much as inside. As usual, I had taken acid and was drinking vodka and tequila. During the evening, I had made a sign stating that every woman must give me a kiss before the evening was done, including the married ones. It was all in good fun, though I never missed an opportunity to kiss a girl!

Around midnight, when everyone was feeling good, Denise, my future sister-in-law, lined up all of the ladies on the deck, and they all went along. About a dozen girls stood in line, and I thought, *Wow! This is great*, and it was. Most of the kisses were just pecks on my cheek until I got to this beautiful redhead at the end of the line, Miss Debbie Poole. I had been around Debbie several times at parties and bars. I had even gotten her in trouble for stolen kisses when other boyfriends were around. But on that night, there were no other boyfriends to interfere, and since she was willing, we had a good, long, sensuous kiss. That kiss turned into the marriage we still have today, and amazingly, I love her more now than I did then. God again had mercy on me by sending me a beautiful woman, both inside and out, whom I did not deserve. As the Beatles song goes, "I'm in love for the first time, don't you know it's gonna last, it's a love that lasts forever, it's a love that has no past."

CHAPTER 12

The Promised Land—Pensacola

"Here I lie in my hospital bed, Tell me, sister morphine
when are you comin' around again? Oh, I don't think I can
wait that long. For you see that I'm not that strong."
—Jagger/Richards

My life was not all roses, for I still had my demons to deal with. In the life of IV drug users, there are many catastrophes and also lots of near disasters as far as their health is concerned. They are always one heartbeat away from tragedy or death. A junkie injects drugs right into the bloodstream, which goes straight to the heart and causes a rush he or she can easily die from.

The first time I had "trash fever" was in 1979. They call it *trash fever* because when injecting drugs, sometimes a microscopic piece of trash, for lack of a better word, gets into the bloodstream along with the dope. The way your body deals with this is by spiking a high fever, perhaps burning it out. All you can do is ride it out, with teeth chattering even though you are burning up. It is the most miserable feeling you can imagine. Junkies understand that they are not privy to health care, as normal people are, so rather than go to the ER, which would be too intrusive anyway, we just take it and hope for the best.

We were so naïve in the 1970s and the 1980s that it's a wonder any of us are still alive, though we are dwindling. We used to think we were taking precautionary measures by cleaning our syringes with water or beer. Even when someone warned me that he had hepatitis, I would ignore the warning if I ran out of needles. Many times I searched the roadsides where I had thrown away old syringes. This was before the days of needle-exchange programs.

It didn't come as much of a surprise when I started turning yellow one day. I was attempting to do a job involving a ladder. Not only could I not climb the ladder, I could not stand up on it. My legs ached worse than they ever had. I thought it was the flu, but when I went to the doctor, he thought it was simply a cold and that I would be better in a few days. However, I continued to feel worse, and I knew by the yellow color of my skin and eyes that something was wrong besides a cold.

Either Debbie or my mother got me an appointment with Dr. Witters, who is still my doctor today. Fortunately, Dr. Witters was not only a good doctor, but he was familiar with the health problems drug addicts deal with. He ordered bloodwork, which revealed that I had hepatitis B. I was immediately hospitalized and quarantined because hepatitis B is contagious. The problem was that I had neither money nor insurance. But Debbie bailed me out. We had fallen in love, and before we knew it, she was caught up in my addiction almost as much as me. She worked on a post-surgical unit at Donelson Hospital and was able to sign me in. Miraculously, that was the only time my liver functions were high, and again, by the grace of God, I did not contract the chronic hepatitis C that so many others have. Actually, it was years later when hepatitis C became an epidemic, but back then, we were ignorant about it.

By 1984 and 1985, my life was spiraling out of control. I was stealing from my family and Debbie, borrowing money when I could, and selling the few possessions I had left. I had bottomed out again and was lost and hopeless. Yet I still clung to the idea that dope would fix it. I had forgotten about God, and I don't think I even prayed. Thank God, other people were still praying for me.

I got the crazy idea that if I just went somewhere else, everything would be okay. My friend Greg and his wife had moved to Pensacola, Florida, and since the healthiest I had been was when I was around him, I thought he could help me again. Greg could fix me. He did not do dope, so he would be a good influence. How delusional I was. I easily forgot the real problem: that I was a drug addict, plain and simple. Responsibility had always been a dirty word with me, and it was much easier to put the burden on someone else.

Debbie and her family were sick of me. In fact, everyone I knew was sick of me. They didn't care where I went, as long as I went somewhere. So I jumped in my old 1971 Dodge Dart, which was rusted out and used more oil than gas. It was around Christmas, and I called up Greg to tell him I was coming, so I was all set. Debbie and my mother put together a few dollars for the trip. Actually, I was looking for a shot of dope for the road. I had a great-looking winter jacket that I loved, which I sold for twenty dollars. That hurt, but I reasoned that I wouldn't need it in Florida anyway. I was so sick and sad at the prospect of leaving everyone I knew and loved, for the uncertainty of what might lay ahead. I was like a child going out in the world with no life skills.

I managed to get a couple of Dilaudids for the trip, but even that did not help the sick, sad feeling as I left Debbie's condo on that cold winter's day. I headed down the interstate on a wing and a prayer, cognizant of the possibility that my old car could break down at any time and knowing for sure that I was going to be dope sick a long way from home. I made it from gas station to gas station, burning a quart of oil about every hundred miles. I did my last shot in Alabama and then started running on coffee, Dilaudid, and adrenaline, dreading the withdrawals that were on the way, but I was headed for the Promised Land: Pensacola.

Well, it turned out that Pensacola was not exactly the Promised Land. I was sick but hopeful as I dreamed of getting with Greg and going back to work with him in the nightclub business. I was trying to get there before I ran out of money or my car died. This was before there were cellphones, so I didn't call Greg until I got to town. There was no answer. I called again with the same result. Finally, his wife answered, rather rudely, and told me that Greg was not home. She didn't know where he was, nor did she care. It seems they'd had a big fight sometime between my Nashville departure and my Florida arrival. Because I didn't have a backup plan, I was scared; I was really on my own.

The only free public place I had found to go was a mall, so I went there with the hope that Greg would be home later that day. Ironically, it was Christmas, and there I was, surrounded by families who seemed happy. This naturally depressed me even more. For someone who compared his insides to others' outsides, I was heavily overmatched, especially when everyone was in the Christmas spirit, while I was hopeless and at the end of the road. I didn't know what I would do if Greg did not return. I hadn't thought that far ahead.

I had twenty dollars to my name, and I was faced with a dilemma. I could try to cop in a strange town's projects, which every junkie can sniff out, or I could attempt to make it home, where I knew how to score. I could stay at the mission in Pensacola, but if I had to sleep in a mission, I would rather it be at home. Since I knew where to cop in Nashville, I headed back there. Even though twenty dollars would not be enough to score, I didn't care. I would find a way. What happened when I got back was one of the most frightening events of my life.

I had been getting my drugs off Douglas Avenue in East Nashville from some young guys who carried guns. They were not users, just sellers, and it was not a good idea to mess with them. A few years earlier, I had been ripped off by a dealer in a place we called "the alley." I had a fifty-dollar bill and was going to hand it to him as he gave me the pill. He tried to snatch the bill, but I held onto it. It ripped in half, so I got no dope, and he got no money. However, I kept my half of the bill and remembered it when I went looking for drugs that day. I had a dollar bill that I taped to the half of the fifty, thinking I would just show the fifty-dollar side. So, I walked up to these young, armed dope dealers in a bad neighborhood, intending to rip them off. Desperation is an amazing thing. That's when the true animal instincts in a junkie come out.

Most of the time I copped by driving up, like a drive-through, but with these guys I had to get out and go into a yard. I got the pill and handed the money to them. Before I got to the car, they discovered that they had been had and yelled for me to stop. I jumped in my car and spun out of there. They decided to chase me, and it was a miracle they didn't catch me because they were in a late-model Buick that could have caught up with my old car easily. I had just gotten to the Silliman Evans Bridge when I saw them gaining on me.

Thankfully, there was enough traffic for me to weave in and

out of it. I had that old car screaming, with oil belching out of the exhaust at about a hundred miles per hour. I was too afraid to worry about the police. At least, *they* wouldn't shoot me. I got off at Fessler's Lane, and after dodging down side streets, I finally lost them. As sick and scared as I was, it did not take long for me to remember the pill I had almost died for. I still had my old, crusty syringe, and I went into the bathroom at Shoney's to try and clean it so it wouldn't clog on me. But on top of everything else, I missed half of the shot, due to my poor, messed-up veins. I almost died for that little pill, and I missed half of it. How ironic.

I got up enough nerve to call Debbie, and she let me spend the night. That was the first Christmas when I would be ostracized from my family. I was not welcome, and it was such a sick, hollow feeling that words cannot describe. I had another Christmas like that the next year before things changed. Knowing that my family was right down the road but not being welcome there was a depressing place to be.

CHAPTER 13

The Road to Recovery

"It's amazing, in the blink of an eye you finally seen the light,
It's amazing, and I'm saying a prayer for
the desperate hearts tonight."
—Aerosmith

My second trip to Cumberland Heights in January 1985 became the basis for my recovery. That was when I truly came to understand that I was an addict and all that it implied. It was also the first time that I actually wanted help for more than a day or two. I finally felt like I was understood by people whom I trusted and respected. I was able to say what I thought and how I felt, and I had someone who could interpret it back to me so I didn't feel so crazy. That old treatment center in the country felt like a warm mother's womb. It had plenty of strong coffee and vitamins, especially the B-complex that was all the rage in the eighties. I shared with other addicts (who may or may not have been sincere, but that was none of my business) who cared. For the moment, all was well, and we had a respite from the demons that had driven us to our knees.

I was in detox the first night and sick as a dog. It was a Friday night, and after-care happened that night. A blond fellow came over to my bed and asked about me, and we talked a little. He told me to get on my knees and ask God to remove the desire to use drugs. I had prayed all my life but never on my knees. I started doing that, and whenever I have, God has removed that desire. I still do it today. The reason I tell this story is that I could never find that man during the next thirty days or any time since. Nobody, staff or patients, knew who he was. I know today that he was an angel sent to me at my lowest who told me in the simplest terms what to do. Get on my knees and pray to God. Period.

I first met George Allen there; he was my primary counselor during my stay. He was one of the first people able to see into me and call me on my denial and impulsiveness, though he did it in a way that made me feel like he cared. He knew what an addict's life is like because he was one. He had ended up on a cold concrete step, alone with a bottle and his disease. George had crawled out of his nightmare, gotten sober, and devoted his life to helping others do the same. George did not judge; he just let me know that he knew what was up, but somehow he made me feel good about it. I have quoted him numerous times over the years and have tried to emulate him. He was a gentle man who touched many people and made the world a better place. God rest his soul.

Cumberland Heights was also the first place that involved my family in therapy. My family and I had to deal with the hard feelings that had built up over ten years. Addiction is like an octopus; it reaches out and touches everyone around the addict in a negative way. The saying "No man is an island" is never truer than with addiction. Regardless of how far away you run, you cannot run from those who love you. It was hard for me because I ran back and forth to those who loved me and dragged them down as well. I was a leech, both physically and emotionally. I sucked the life out of people by using them. I was finally able to apologize to Mama, Daddy, and Debbie. In a tear-filled garble, I was finally able to tell my father that he was my hero. Sadly, I had more to go through before I got my life back on track, and it all ended.

I wish that the great experience in Cumberland Heights in 1985 was the end of my struggle, but during the next two years I went downhill after being clean for about ninety days in the spring of 1985. By New Year's Eve of 1985, I was in the Samaritan Center for thirty days and then went on to their halfway house, which was in an almost condemned building next to the residential treatment facility. I remember getting my morning started by having Sanka coffee mixed with hot water from the tap. I made it out of there in a few weeks and even had a roommate and an apartment. I was going to meetings and was eight months' clean, and then I relapsed. I missed Christmas of 1985 and would miss it again in 1986. I was so sick by mid-December that I really wanted to die. I was ostracized by everyone and had nowhere to live. I was a hopeless, pathetic human being.

For some reason, I made a call to Dr. Witters, who had seen me through hepatitis in 1983. I had no money and no insurance, but he saw me and made a phone call to a psychiatrist in Donelson. By the grace of God, she got me admitted into Parthenon Pavilion for detox. She knew enough about addiction to realize that I didn't need another drug, and when I asked her after five days' detox if I could go to an NA meeting, she said yes. That was December 1986, the month I picked up a white surrender chip and meant it from the heart.

They say coincidence is when God chooses to remain anonymous. I would say it is just the opposite: when God reveals truth you can see, if you are searching for it diligently. My proof started with my first NA meeting where David, a former drug buddy, met me when I arrived. I had lost contact with David over the years, like so many other angels I have encountered. I met the group of people who would change and save my life. I found out what is meant by the quote "A true friend is one who is walking in when the rest of the world is walking out." A group of true friends was waiting for me when I walked through the door.

As I mentioned earlier, I had *dabbled* in recovery earlier by going to a few meetings beginning in April 1983, but I was not ready to change at that time. I spent the next three years shuffling through life the best I could. There were not enough drugs in the world to kill the pain that weighed me down. I was getting closer to the breaking point, where I couldn't live with or without drugs. I was hollow on the inside and became totally hopeless. By then, I was aware of NA but could not bring myself to commit to it or anything else.

My worst years were from 1983 through 1985. I was completely without hope or purpose. I was like a vampire who couldn't get enough blood to live on. However, I did manage to start some counseling sessions. At Dede Wallace Center, a therapist named James did not judge me, which was something I desperately needed. I remember poor Debbie going to those sessions with me and waiting outside. This was also the first time she heard me admit I was an addict, although that was like a zebra discovering it had stripes. I wondered if she thought I lived my insane, drug-fueled life because I had nothing better to do. I'm not quite sure what she was thinking at that time, but thank God she didn't overthink it because if she had, she probably would have called it quits, then and there. Sadly, I continued to drag her down with me.

However, the road to recovery was beginning to work for me. I knew that everything depended on me getting straight: my family, my health, my life. It wasn't an easy path to follow, but I was beginning to see some light.

I have been sitting here these last few days reflecting on the more than five thousand meetings I have attended and all the special people I have been blessed to meet along the way, people who still influence me, even those who are no longer with us. I had a wonderful dream the other night starring Richard Hogan, who was one of my oldest friends in the program. In fact, Richard was one of the seven people who started the first NA meeting in Nashville in 1979. I came along four years later and met my first sponsor, Winston Grizzard, who was one of the original seven. In my dream, Richard was still moving about, being his usual charismatic self and the center of attention. I truly loved that man and miss him every day!

The NA program tells us to hang out with the winners, and I believe that is what I have done. When I was on the streets, I hung out with the older, more-experienced addicts so they could show me the ropes, and I have used that same principle in my recovery. I do my best to stay optimistic and have a good time, or what would be the point? I did not get clean to be miserable. In recovery, it's very beneficial to begin learning how to feel content and happy. Our program is about having the freedom to do what we always wanted to do but were afraid—and about becoming the people God intended us to be before our lives were warped by the disease of addiction.

Rick A. and I used to talk about *that feeling* we got in meetings, which I truly believe is the spiritual connection flowing from one addict to another. There is a feeling of empathy that is both given and received. There is always that bobbing head, as people unconsciously acknowledge that they can relate to what is being said.

This Sunday, Debbie and I will celebrate twenty-nine years of marriage, and on Monday, our daughter, Katlyn, will turn twenty-seven. This may not seem like a big deal in the grand scheme of things, but I believe that it's those little things that make up the grand scheme. My life has been such a miracle, a string of ironies that cannot be explained, except through the eyes and handiwork of God. Thirty-plus years ago, I was nearly dead: physically, spiritually, and emotionally. If you had told people what was about to happen in my life back then, they would have told you that you were higher than I was. God was preparing me for the greatest of all adventures. It has not been a smooth ride, and sometimes it's still like a frightening roller-coaster rush. But I have no doubt that God already knew that, and He set the people in place to achieve His ultimate goal for me: my salvation and redemption. My family, wife, daughter, schoolteachers, and coaches have all been a part of His picture, which I was too blind to see.

All I know is that I was lost and dying, and I asked God for help. Although I was a tough case, He saved me. He knew I needed extra help, and He led me to a bunch of drug addicts. These were the same people I had been around for years; the only difference was that these addicts were clean and had found a new way of life. I was drowning, and they were the life boat. They prepared me for the next phase of my storybook life with Deb and Kate and all the other marvelous people who would come into my life during the next three decades.

Looking back, I realize I have been under God's grace the whole time. I have no other explanation. I have been more blessed and pulled out of the fire more times than I can remember. In the book of Galatians, the Apostle Paul said, "May I never boast except in the cross of our Lord Jesus Christ." God touched my life and guided me. I have tried to drive my life so many times and have always ended up in the ditch, and yet I have not only survived but thrived. I believe He saved me for a reason, though only He really knows what that reason is.

God does not make junk. He can take the most twisted wreckage of a life and make it new again. My many scars, both inside and out, make God's handiwork even more beautiful. Think of how Christ spent that ugly, grotesque, torturous time on the cross and how He became the most perfect example of love ever displayed. My story is but a microcosm compared to that of Christ, yet the story of His grace plays out all around us every day. We can see it if we open our eyes and hearts. Sometimes I struggle and feel like I don't deserve God's love. Then I remember God's Amazing Grace!

Sometimes I feel like the main character in the book of Job in the Bible. Job, a prosperous farmer, was a righteous man. God allowed Satan to test Job because Satan claimed that Job loved God only because he was wealthy and everything was going well with him. I have considered that on the day I was born, Satan told Jesus that he would take this little choirboy, turn his world upside-down, and turn him into a modern-day leper: a junkie. The wonderful news is that Jesus answered Satan and told him that He would have the final word on my fate. Thank God for that!

I have found great strength and comfort recently in the team of people who have been supporting my family through my time of illness and financial problems. I always pray to God, and He answers. I am overwhelmed and humbled by all that people do for us. I am also grateful for all the people who have always been on my side, rooting for me since I was a young boy in church and school. They encouraged me when I played baseball, the sport I loved as a boy, and they inspired me in my later life. I am also very thankful to the members of Narcotics Anonymous who have been there since my first meeting. NA was my first real taste of empathy, and I know it comes from the heart, rather than the head. I was taken along a path toward healing and restoration to a point where I could return to my family and church.

I believe in angels and demons, and I know that I was influenced for many years by demons, mostly with my cooperation. I also know that I have been protected and surrounded by angels, or I would not still be here. I have also been helped by people who, though they might not be actual angels, have blessed me in angelic ways. That's why I'm aware that it is my responsibility to give back what I can and to be empathetic to anyone who appears to be struggling. I did not end up where I was on purpose, and I must assume that most other people don't either.

All these years later, I occasionally have an inner debate on whether I am forgiven for all of the wrong I have done. I am hardheaded, and Satan loves to play on my weaknesses. However, I believe we all have moments of doubt, and this is just part of being human. God has proved Himself to me during my lifetime. I pray daily for God to forgive me, and He alone can judge my heart and motives.

I remember what someone told me in a meeting when I brought up the same issue. This man came up to me after the meeting and asked whether I believed that God had forgiven me. I stuttered, "I guess so." He asked, "If God has forgiven you, how can you put yourself above Him by not forgiving yourself?" which is what I suppose it comes down to. He made a logical point. But, like other people, I am aware of my sins, both past and present, and sometimes I can let them get me down. I look at all I am going through physically and mentally, and sometimes I feel like I deserve it. But my family does not because they are suffering right along with me. My point is that even though life can be very challenging at times, I know deep in my heart that God has grace and mercy for me. I sorely need His peace that is beyond all understanding! As I mentioned earlier, we all have our moments of doubt and pain.

A big part of my recovery and ministry came about through my involvement with civic organizations and clubs. I became involved with the Mount Juliet Chamber of Commerce and was on its board of directors. I was also in the Mt. Juliet Rotary Club and Leadership Wilson. I made many contacts through them, and therefore many people heard my story. In that way, I was able to help out when a friend or a family member was struggling with addiction. I became that person's liaison to the recovery community. It may seem strange, but when people are affected by another's addiction, many do not know where to turn for help.

Working with these organizations and people in the community was a strange experience because a lot of those individuals had known me since I was a child, and some were familiar with my crazier times. But it was great. It made me feel like part of my community again. Through the Rotary Club, I was able to organize a fundraiser with Mount Juliet's first 5K race. I had been running in races for a few years and had always wanted one in my hometown. We began in 1990 and held races for the next five years, right in the heart of Mount Juliet.

As I have said, it has not been all rosy since my decision to give my life back to God. Everything came crashing down on January 25, 2019. The phone rang around midnight, which always scares me anyway, and I heard Debbie talking to my mother. My mother said that my nephew Jeremy was gone and that the paramedics were either at her home, where Jeremy was living at the time, or on the way. We sped over there to find the paramedics in the driveway with Jeremy in the back of the vehicle. A paramedic was bagging him so he could breathe. I asked whether he was dead, and the paramedic said no, but he could not breathe on his own. Mama was so upset that she had to stay home. We called my brother, Jerry, told him what had happened and to meet us at the hospital. That was the first scene of a three- or four-day tragedy that ended in Jeremy's death on Tuesday, January 29, at about 5:00 p.m.

As I looked at one of his pictures at the memorial service, I wondered, *How did I let you down, kid?* Did I not say or do something, the one thing that might have saved his life? Did I not try to convince myself or the family to stop enabling him? The thing I always preach to a family is that they have to be tough in their love, instead of loving addicts to death by continuing to enable them. Otherwise, they will be standing over their loved one's casket, just as I was doing. Of all the tasks we are assigned on earth, figuring out the best way to deal with a practicing addict is one of the most daunting.

Addicts learn early on how to manipulate those who love them. At times, they will make you feel like you are being cold-hearted and that you are abandoning them. But if you really love them, you must look past their addiction and realize that giving in to their every whim is not helping, it's hurting. The sad fact is that most addicts do not have a long life span, and the time that an active addict is alive is spent living like an animal. We drown slowly but surely, dragging down those who love us with us. The devil must have a special cheering section when an addict crosses that line. I feel sick thinking about my own disease and how it has affected so many people who cared for and loved me. Sadly, the only difference between Jeremy and me is that I lived long enough to get out alive. Only by the grace of God am I still alive, though I am haunted by survivor's remorse. It has been a recurring theme every time I go to someone whose loved one has passed, and I wonder whether they are looking at me, thinking, *Why are you still here and my loved one has gone?* I've been to too many funerals and spoken at many, trying to comfort the families and the friends. Through it all, Jeremy's belief in the Lord never wavered. John 3:16 was written for Jeremy and his sweet soul. He is finally home.

CHAPTER 14

God's Gift of the 12-Step Fellowships

Thank you, Bill W. and Dr. Bob, Founders of
AA, and Jimmy K., Founder of NA.
"Let this circle represent what we can do
together, that none of us can alone."
—Common NA saying before the closing prayer

I am writing this chapter with the most thought and care that I can muster. It is about my thirty-plus years as a member of a 12-step group called Narcotics Anonymous. I speak only for myself; these are my opinions and experiences. Anonymity and confidentiality are the cornerstones that make up the foundation of all 12-step groups, which began with Alcoholics Anonymous in 1933. Do yourself a favor and read AA's history and the stories of its founders, Bill Wilson and Dr. Bob. Many excellent books and films tell their stories personally and that of AA as a whole. I'm afraid we have gotten away from the spirit of anonymity these days, but I will save that for the next book!

I attended my first meeting in April 1983, as I related earlier. Though I have not been clean consistently for the last thirty-five years, NA has been the foundation of my personal recovery. I floundered in and out for the first three years, and then, during a stay in Parthenon Pavilion, I was allowed to attend a meeting outside on Christmas Eve of 1986. That night I called a friend in the program, Holly, and asked her for a ride to that meeting, and she kindly consented. I did not ask her for money, a job, or a place to live. I just asked for a ride to a meeting to help me get on the road to recovery, and like every time I have asked an NA member to help me in my recovery, they have said yes. Recovery is a team sport; there is only we, not I. There is a saying in all 12-step programs: "We found we could do together what none of us could do alone." I picked up a white surrender chip that night and stayed clean for the next ten years. Our third-step prayer goes, "God, take my will and my life, guide me in my recovery, and show me how to live." That says it all.

I got a sponsor, a person who is willing to help guide people through the 12 steps. I learned to trust my sponsor with my fears, secrets, and hopes. He became the most important person in my recovery process. I was blessed with two great sponsors. I started going to meetings every day, and even though it is suggested that a newcomer go to ninety meetings in ninety days, I was so scared that I went to more than one meeting a day during the first eighteen months. I totally immersed myself in the NA program, and everything I did involved some activity with NA members. Some people make fun of us and say it is a cult, that we are brainwashed. I reply that my brain needed a good washing! Another great saying that has stuck with me is: "You can't think your way into right acting, but you can act your way into right thinking." That can be as simple as making a phone call, going to a meeting, or getting on my knees to pray. The point is that trying to "think" my way out of the insanity in my head leads me into a vicious circle of more insane thinking. As I immersed myself in the recovery process by going into jails and treatment centers to carry the NA message and working the steps with my sponsor, I found myself moving further away from that old life. I learned how to live a minute, an hour, and then a day at a time not using drugs. The physical cessation of drugs is not easy, but it is simple. Learning how to live a productive life in society while not using drugs is a different matter.

Even though I had been raised in church, I had run so far away from it that I did not know how to get back to God. It's funny that a recovering addict could help me when a preacher or a counselor could not. I had found empathy from people who were just like me. I was not crazy, immoral, or evil. I saw God doing for people what they could not do for themselves. I saw lives being restored and families starting to heal. I was able, through the steps, to look at myself for the first time. It was uncomfortable but not impossible. There is truth in the saying "An unexamined life is not worth living." I could see and name my shortcomings, which the Apostle Paul said we all suffer from. All of us fall short and have particular defects, which are sometimes best shared with others and particularly with our sponsor, in whom we can confide things we are not comfortable sharing in groups.

The biggest step I took when I was about eighteen months' clean was being able to actually look at my parents, Debbie, and others I had harmed and make amends to them. Just being clean had repaired a lot of the damage, but I had to tell them I was wrong and to "clean up my side of the street," as they say. Although my drug use, criminal behavior, immoral living, and everything else that went with a drug addict's lifestyle took me far away from my spiritual roots, I still had morals and ethics way down deep inside of me because of how I was nurtured and raised. The Bible says that if you bring a child up in the way of the Lord, but he still goes astray, he will know to return to the fold. I try to live the 9th step, the amends step, every day to society as a whole. I can never repay society for the damage I did over many years, but I can try.

My story has a lot in common with the parable of the Prodigal Son, who knew that even while he was envious of what the pigs were eating, there was a better way: the way of his Father. My earthly father was a great representative for my Father in heaven. God wants us to admit our wrongs and come home. You really can come home again. My earthly father, Harry, would have laughed at my comparing him to God, but he was always there for me, except when he wanted to kill me! He got in my face one time in 1978 and, with his beet-red face and clenched fist, threatened to hit me because, as he said, I was killing my mother, and I was. Many people in recovery don't come from good homes, but I did. I had no one to blame for my behavior but me. No abuse of any kind, just a spoiled-rotten kid with a drug problem and disease that led me in a vicious cycle.

Narcotics Anonymous is growing tremendously, both in Nashville and worldwide. The fellowship doubled in size worldwide from the 1980s to the 1990s. We grew like crazy in Nashville. When I started attending meetings in 1983, there were only five or six real meetings a week. During the next ten years, it grew to more than a hundred meetings a week in Middle Tennessee. We were welcomed into the local treatment centers and prisons to bring what were called *hospital and institution meetings* to inmates and patients. NA really started growing up and was no longer the stepchild of AA. AA was a Godsend in 1933, and we are eternally grateful, but by 1953, I believe God saw the time was right for a group to help people with the overall disease of addiction and not focus on only one substance. Jimmy K. and a small group founded NA in California in 1953, and, as they say, the rest is history. The 12-step format has now expanded into many areas, including gambling, overeating, debtors, sexual addiction, and many more. All of the programs owe profound gratitude to the founders of Alcoholics Anonymous, which is actually based on Biblical principles.

The next ten years would alter and set my path for the rest of my life. I was able to marry my beautiful lady, Debbie, in 1989. I got back into my real estate career and started my construction business with the help of my father and my brother, Jerry. Our very first incarnation in the remodeling business, we called the Grass Group, after our last name, Snodgrass. I have always wondered whether the IRS or some other government entity flagged that name.

The most important event to happen was about two years after Debbie and I married: we had Katlyn. That child is twenty-eight, as of this writing, and she is a force to be reckoned with. As she grew up, it was a trip for an immature recovering addict to butt heads with an immature, hardheaded child. I love her beyond words and stand amazed at the strong woman she has become. She is an advocate for abused women and children, and if you need someone to fight for you, she is the person. Her heart is the biggest thing about her and fills her with passion and compassion. The world will be a better place in the future because of Katlyn Shea Snodgrass!

During the first year of our marriage, Debbie and I started attending Madison Church of Christ, which is located in Madison, Tennessee, a suburb of Nashville. At the time, it was one of the largest Churches of Christ in the world. Every Sunday, more than two thousand folks attended worship there. On our first anniversary, Debbie was baptized by Steve Flatt, our preacher, and we also placed membership that day. As Ray Wilson told me, "God can see a whole lot further out than we can," and He sure could because neither Debbie nor I had any idea where the next twenty-nine years would take us. Madison Church of Christ would become a major partner in our lives. I got involved with the Madison Children's Home and Domestic Violence Program early on. I became a board member and eventually the chairman of the board. I worked with a great man, Nick Boone, who truly had a servant's heart. Nick was in charge and changed many children's and women's lives for the better. I also gradually let people at Madison know that I was involved in the recovery community and wanted to help anyone who needed help. Ray Wilson and Bobby McElhiney, both elders, asked me to become a deacon in the church. My area of ministry was helping anyone with a substance abuse problem at Madison. This was a profound and visionary act for the church to acknowledge the problem of addiction and to offer solutions to those who suffered with the disease. I knew I had found another home, first NA and now Madison.

Madison Church of Christ has played a huge role in my life. Months after my 1995 surgery debacle, I was hooked on the narcotics. I had my foundation in NA but knew I needed a safe place to detox. I was bull-headed and did not want to go to a treatment center for medical detox. My friends at Madison Church had been there for us during my illness, and God gave us the idea to call a strong Christian friend, David Hardin, and tell him what we were trying to do. I told David that I needed to be protected from myself until I could physically withdraw from the narcotics. The folks at church knew my story and had fully supported me in my ministry, but they did not know what I was going through.

David (I believe with the help of the Holy Spirit) began mobilizing men to hang out with me in a hotel for a few days while I detoxed. Again, I was usually the one organizing this type of thing. Looking back, the situation was like a surgeon who needed surgery but was physically unable to do it, although he was able to guide someone to perform the surgery on himself. That is what I felt like as I guided these men on how to treat me. I told them not to trust me and not to let me out of their sight.

They set up a schedule and, for four days or so, stayed with me. During the evening, a small group would come up, some with their children, and I would share what I was going through. I more or less gave them a quick primer on addiction and withdrawal; I was a very sick man. These men would hug me, put their hands on me, and pray over me. I would like to think that they got as much out of the experience as I did. After one of the evening prayer sessions, as we talked and shared with one another, one of our ministers said something that got a real reaction from the group. He had felt and witnessed what was going on in that room, and he blurted out, "I'll bet the devil is enraged about what we are doing." We looked at one another and laughed because that was fully what we intended to do: thwart the plans of the devil! I hope he was very upset because he roars like a lion, but I had a team of lions and prayer warriors who had come to do battle, and we won that battle with the help of Jesus and His Spirit!

The men involved still talk about that event after all these years, and it further enhanced my ministry and the foundation for what was coming: the Amazing Grace Recovery Program. Yet once again it came after I was humbled by the thorn in my side. Once again I humbled myself and said that powerful word: *help*. I'm drowning, and I can't save myself.

A funny thing happened in church a few years later when Katlyn was about ten. She was sitting beside me at the end of worship when someone walked up front during the invitation and asked for prayers and help with a drug problem. Well, as I always did, I grabbed a piece of paper and wrote my name and phone number. I also explained that I was a recovering addict who would like to help him. I was preparing to go up after church and meet this individual and offer him my information. Katlyn had been watching me write, and even though she had seen me go to a meeting every night and occasionally went with me, this was the first time the light bulb went off in her little head about what her daddy was. Before I could go up front, she looked up at me and asked so innocently, "You're a drugaholic?" Debbie and I just laughed and still do to this day, as she fully understands her daddy is a "drugaholic!"

CHAPTER 15

The Amazing Grace Recovery Program

And so began the roots and the foundation of what would officially become, in 2012, the Amazing Grace Recovery Program, a coming together of the lifesaving properties of the 12-step programs and the soul-saving, life-renewing nature of Jesus Christ. The spiritual principles already available to every person involved in 12-step recovery moved into a full-blown spiritual experience of a life filled with the Holy Spirit. I finally had a path to talk openly about the 12 steps coming directly out of the scriptures, and I could show the recovery community and the Christian community that we were actually on the same page.

Let me say here that the 12-step groups need their independence to carry out their primary purpose, which is to help the suffering addict find a way to get clean and stay clean. They need to keep the concepts of "Higher Power" and "Power greater than themselves." Believe me, when an addict like me crawls into a 12-step meeting, just hearing the words "God as you understand Him" is a shock to the system. You feel like such a worthless excuse for a human being that you understand the devil, at that point, much more than God. The disease of addiction is cunning, baffling, and powerful. It is a big enough goal of recovery programs to help addicts get clean and stay clean. We, in the 12-step recovery communities, need the prayers of everyone, but we need to stay focused on our primary purpose: helping the addict who is still suffering.

The name Amazing Grace came from two thought processes. The Amazing Grace Bible Class was broadcast on TV for a number of years from the Madison Church of Christ. Ira North led the class, and Nick Boone was the song leader. Amazing Grace was in the DNA at Madison, and so I thought that since our group would be based there, the name was appropriate. The word *grace* has a deep meaning in the recovery community. You will rarely attend a 12-step meeting where someone doesn't mention they are clean or alive only by the grace of God. They share that only by His grace were they able to survive the life of addiction.

Many of the people who attend 12-step meetings do not attend church, but they understand grace much better than many Christians. They understand grace on a gut level. They have stared into the abyss of utter destruction from their disease. They are thankful that because of their recovery efforts, they were able to avoid jail, insanity, or death. They got so much more on the positive side: life, health, and soundness of mind. They advanced from living daily nightmares to being responsible, productive members of society.

Every day the benefits of recovery are being displayed throughout society. The active part of addiction affects everyone negatively; the recovery process affects every person and segment of society positively. The Drug Court program that was created in Nashville by Judge Norman is a shining example of what can happen when addiction is treated as a disease. Addicts are now able to receive treatment for their problem, rather than punishment alone. They still have to pay for their crimes in the Drug Court system, but when they walk out of jail, they are potentially on the road to rehabilitation. Judge Norman's Drug Court is a model that is followed throughout the nation.

The second reason the Amazing Grace Recovery Program was created was to complement and add to the established recovery programs already in existence, not to replace them. Those seeking recovery have these groups available to help them get clean and recover. We wanted to help in their journey by emphasizing the extraordinary and miraculous power available to them when they develop a relationship with God through Jesus Christ.

God is spoken of freely in 12-step meetings but in a very open and general way, so as not to offend people or run them off before they can really hear the recovery message. I always preach that what I say in a 12-step meeting should be geared more to the newcomer than the old timer. The disease is always looking for a way to block a newcomer from hearing about staying clean and how to do it. Many using addicts have had a bad history with organized religion, which makes them skeptical about spiritual matters. No one knows addiction, and therefore recovery, the way another recovering addict does.

One night I walked outside a meeting place located at Green Hill Church of Christ, and my friend Robert asked me about God and Jesus. He was having a hard time with the God concept, as so many newcomers do. I started sharing with him about my relationship with Jesus, and before long, both he and his mother were baptized. That was one of the first examples of what I wanted to accomplish with Amazing Grace Recovery.

Incidentally, that meeting place at Green Hill Church of Christ, which they so graciously allowed us to start using in 1993, was the same space where I attended Sunday school classes as a teenager.

Another irony was that a bunch of recovering addicts drinking coffee could get through to me about spirituality better than the well-meaning teachers I had when I was younger. Of course, it was not their fault. It was like I've always said: I have a hearing problem. I hear what I want to hear and only hear the truth when I surrender and become willing to listen. The old saying "When the pupil is ready, the teacher will appear" is certainly true.

I love the concept of irony. For example, when I was eight years old, I attended church camp with my Aunt Margaret, who was the camp nurse. She sent a note home to my mother, saying how much I was enjoying camp and that I had told her I wanted to be a preacher when I grew up. My mother still has the note. I didn't take the usual course to becoming a preacher, and I do not profess to be one now, but I definitely have a ministry. The irony was that after every near-fatal car crash or overdose, I would hear words like "God must be saving you for a reason" or "God is not done with you yet" coming from a well-meaning Christian friend. I would blow it off and go get high again, but now I know how prophetic those words were.

The Amazing Grace Recovery Program became a free-standing 501(c)(3) nonprofit organization in 2012 and remains so today. We began meeting every Wednesday evening on the Madison campus and started a smaller group on Sunday morning. We use Christian recovery meditation books and *The Life Recovery Bible*, which are excellent guides to help us discuss everyday recovery problems and situations. I sometimes feel inadequate guiding the discussions, but God always leads the way in our group and in the individual members' lives. We have monthly pizza parties and holiday parties. T-shirts for summer and hoodies for winter have become a mainstay. The words *Amazing Grace* just happened to work perfectly to fill in the Sign of the Cross, so that became our logo for all our outerwear. It's *amazing* how that design just came into my head because I am not a graphic artist. I receive many compliments on our shirts and hoodies when I am out in public. It is always a smile and a "Really like your shirt." Sometimes the shirts will elicit a conversation, and I can share our story and offer my name and number in case the person ever needs our help.

The classes and the group are a big part of what we do, but every week I am a resource for addicts, as well as their families. I speak to groups all the time and will ask how many know someone who is in trouble with addiction. It can be a friend, a loved one, or a coworker. The response is almost always unanimous, but then when I ask how many know where to get help, very few hands go up. That's where I come in. I call it the silent ministry. Denial and shame are the first symptoms in the addict, the family member, or the friend. When I get calls, people are hesitant to open up at first, but as they begin to talk, the floodgates open. They let it out and tell me their stories, eventually asking for help and direction. There is powerful support available when someone uses the word *Help*! It is one of the strongest words in the English language. When we cry out to God or to a person who encourages and supports us, these are the first signs of surrender, the first acknowledgment that we are drowning and dying. That is why suicide is so prevalent among addicts—because even though we may have a pulse, we are not really living, just existing. The first step says, "We admitted we were powerless over our addiction." Everyone in my stratosphere knew I was powerless; I was the last to admit it, the last to realize my total lack of any control.

The scary part is what I call "the iceberg theory," the idea that addicts are so good at hiding and deception that what friends and family actually see in their lives is what the addicts did not intend for them to see. The addicts made mistakes as they got worse or got caught, and that hidden part of their life was revealed. We only see maybe 1 percent of the iceberg, and the rest is hidden. Think about the Titanic! Another reason I tell parents and spouses to follow their first instincts is that if it doesn't look or smell right, it's probably not right! Rarely have I seen folks act *too* quickly when they are concerned about an addict or someone they think is in trouble. It is usually the opposite; they have received that dreaded late-night phone call and regret their inaction the rest of their lives. An addict's actions and the consequences on their loved ones can reach out far beyond their last breath. Too many family members and friends are haunted for years and decades.

I wish I had kept better records of all the phone calls and the cries for help I have received, usually from family members. I try to explain to them what is going on because most of the time, family and friends are too close to the situation to be objective. They are already damaged and scarred and may not even know it. They are already caught up in the tentacles of addiction. In a war, it would be termed *collateral damage*. Many times, they will not fully acknowledge how deep they are in and how much help they themselves really need. I leave their situation in God's hands temporarily, until I can try to get the addict the help he or she needs. That might be treatment, medical detox, or even a halfway house. Almost always, we are dealing with folks who have no insurance or money. That starts the process of joining with some really dedicated people to work the system and get them state grant money, which is set aside for the treatment centers that are mostly nonprofit. Another irony with this disease, which is so deadly and costly, is that even when people want help, it's sometimes necessary to work through some red tape to get them help. I suggest doing whatever it takes to get the addict help, especially when he or she is finally willing. I will leave it at that.

The Amazing Grace Recovery Program has several goals: helping people get clean, aiding them in their *ongoing* recovery, making recovery fun, and adding completeness to their recovery experience. The ultimate goal of Amazing Grace Recovery is to give recovering people an avenue to develop their spiritual lives and to be saved eternally with Jesus Christ. When Jesus was starting His ministry, He chose Matthew the tax collector, Peter the foul-mouthed fisherman with an anger problem, and Thomas the eternal skeptic. I sometimes joke that if Jesus were starting his ministry today, he would find a 12-step meeting and pick from some of the most defective, fallen people who are at the same time some of the best, kindest people you will ever have the privilege of meeting. These people have an intimate knowledge of the concept of grace. They know they did not get what they deserved because they are free and alive. They are receiving so much more than they could have hoped for in the form of recovery. I have had the honor of knowing and loving some of the best folks ever, and they have come from Sunday school classes to 12-step meetings, from churches to prison settings. We are all fallen and broken; it's just that the sins of addicts are more pronounced and out in the public square.

As I mentioned earlier, in 1987, my mama and daddy attended my one-year birthday for being clean. At her very first NA meeting, Mama said, "This is how church ought to be." What she meant was that addicts share openly and honestly about how damaged they are, and they share their burdens with one another, just as the Bible tells us to do.

CHAPTER 16

Embracing Faith and Courage to Handle Health Challenges

"Won't you look down upon me, Jesus?
You gotta help me make a stand,
You just gotta see me through another day.
My body's aching and my time is at hand,
I won't make it any other way."
—James Taylor

I feel compelled to address my health history as it shapes and shadows my life from 1995 to the present. In 1995, I had what I considered would be a simple gallbladder surgery. It went horribly wrong and changed the course of my life. During the laparoscopic surgery, an extra hepatic (liver) duct that was not supposed to be there was hiding behind the cystic (gallbladder) duct and was cut/severed at the same time my gallbladder was removed. Unfortunately, no one realized this had occurred, and I was sent home to recover. I immediately began having severe pain and nausea, and after several tests it was discovered that my abdominal cavity was filled with bile from my liver. I looked eight months' pregnant! They drained 2 liters (think coke bottle) from

105

my abdomen. It took thirty days of pain, weakness, and multiple hospitalizations, procedures, and another surgery to discover what was causing this problem. I lost 28 pounds and was acutely ill.

I was transferred to Vanderbilt's liver transplant service, and surgery was scheduled the next day—not for a liver transplant, but to repair and reconnect the secondary hepatic duct and re-route other ducts and vessels. I was in a very weakened state and fearful of dying. The surgery lasted approximately seven hours, and, for my family, it seemed like forever. My recovery took months, but I did recover . . . or so I thought. But then I started having pain and fevers with frequent infections. That set up years of invasive procedures to reopen my duct and install stents. I have probably had at least forty outpatient procedures in the last twenty-four years on that little duct! All along, my family has had to watch me go through the physical and mental side effects of my health issues, while they also endured the mental and emotional anguish.

My guilt still extends to my daughter, who as a little girl wanted daddy to be there when she came home from school, but frequently I was in the hospital instead. Katlyn thought all along, in that little mind of hers, that it was somehow her fault that I had to keep going back into the hospital. Katlyn was only four years old when all the medical issues started. She has endured this burden practically her entire life. Jesus warns us not to harm these little ones, and I was harming Katlyn without even knowing it. When Katlyn was in the seventh grade, she came home from school and said she was not going back. She was so lost and scared, it broke my heart. So, the homeschooling began. Now, if you know my lovely wife and me, we are not exactly homeschooling material. Debbie referred to it as self-schooling, not homeschooling, but that would fill another whole other chapter!

In 2003, after my many bouts with sepsis (infection in the blood) from e-coli and duct blockages, it was finally decided to remove part of my liver to get rid of my abnormal ductwork, which continued to cause trouble. Dr. Burns, to whom I owe so much, contacted the liver transplant surgeon at Vanderbilt, and a liver resection was planned to remove 70 percent of my liver. One of the miracles of the human body is that the liver is the only organ that can regenerate itself. The liver is a very vascular organ and, as such, is easy to bleed, so the surgery was high risk, and it took more than eight hours. The doctor said later that he spent the first two hours staring at my liver, trying to decide exactly how to perform the intricate surgery. It appeared that I had some abnormal ductwork inside my liver as well. After my first surgery, they discovered that I had horseshoe kidneys (my kidneys are attached in a horseshoe shape), and now this. I am abnormal, as I'd always thought!

So that's what happened in 2003, and, of course, I experienced problems and setbacks. I believe Murphy's Law (anything that can go wrong will go wrong) was written for me. Whether it was a procedure or surgery, if a complication could happen, it did. I developed an abscess on my liver, and my doctor was out of town. Someone else tried to drain it, but the surgeon punctured my lung and introduced bacteria from my liver abscess into my lung. This required two additional surgeries to scrape the bacteria out of my lung, resulting in three more weeks in the hospital. I was sent home with a chest tube and IV antibiotics. I am so thankful that my wonderful wife is a nurse! After I finally recovered from the surgeries, I actually had four or five years of fairly good health.

Then, sometime in 2009, I started getting those symptoms again: lethargy, nausea, pain, fever, no stamina. At first, we didn't think it was problems with my ductwork, but in 2014, I had an endoscopy performed. Lo and behold, it showed some blockage in my common bile duct. It did not warrant a stent at that time. I was sick intermittently for the next two years and decided to get a second opinion from a GI doctor at another hospital. That was a BIG MISTAKE. We gave him my detailed medical/surgical history, and he was concerned that the duct was blocked. He wanted to perform an ERCP to confirm this and perhaps insert a stent. How I wish I could stop the story here, but this is where the nightmare of my medical history kicks into overdrive.

February 10, 2016, is a day that changed everything in my family's life. More than three years later, I sit here and still get sick thinking about it. I talked to a therapist about having PTSD, and she said the only problem with that diagnosis is the "post" part because I am still in the "present" with it. I am forever damaged by it.

My anatomy was not normal, apparently not at birth and certainly not at this point in my life. After all the procedures and the surgeries, my abdominal cavity and everything connected with it were anything but normal. It was imperative to proceed with caution. Our firm belief is that this doctor was anything but cautious. Our feelings have been substantiated by multiple medical personnel. Suffice it to say that things went terribly wrong again. I awoke in the recovery area in immense pain. I was admitted to the hospital, and by the next morning, I was in the ICU with pancreatitis.

My condition went downhill quickly, and within a few days I was unresponsive. I was then diagnosed with acute infectious necrotizing pancreatitis . . . the worst form of pancreatitis. I had all the ICU bells and whistles attached to me, except a respirator. Thankfully, I could breathe on my own. My body was inflamed, especially on the right side of my abdomen, my hip, my back, and down my leg and foot. The areas were hot pink and on fire to the touch. My body blew up like a blowfish, and infection raged throughout my body. And my pancreas . . . well, it was really ticked off. The pancreas secretes enzymes that break down proteins and fat. When it gets angry, as mine did, those enzymes are released inside the pancreas, instead of outside the pancreas in the bile ducts, and the pancreas literally starts "eating" itself. During the next three weeks, I was in the ICU with only a few moments of being lucid. I thought at one point that I was in the Dairy Queen. The mind works in mysterious ways when you're sedated.

I was told daily it was a roller-coaster ride as to whether I would make it through the day. If not for the excellent care I received at St Thomas Hospital, I believe I would not be writing this today. I want to give a big shout-out to Megan (my angel), an exceptional nurse practitioner, the great nurses, and the hospitalist. It hurts me and makes me sick and angry that my wife, daughter, and mother had to see me lying in that bed, day after day, wondering whether any moment would be the last time they would see me on this side of eternity. My family cried an ocean of tears for me, and I'm thankful for each day I have to make it up to them. I was finally discharged from the hospital after five weeks. I was ALIVE, and I was HOME!

About ten days after my discharge, I was on my way back to the ER. I had a fever, persistent vomiting, and awful pain. Debbie and I decided to seek care at Vanderbilt, and I was admitted under the care of a trauma surgeon. I had three bilomas in my belly; one was as big as a blown-up balloon! Bilomas are collections of bile fluid in the abdomen, usually from leaks or trauma. When they become infected, they are more critical to treat. I had another surgery to insert two large tubes to drain them. After the surgery, I vomited repeatedly and was unable to take in any kind of nutrition. One day the nurses came into my room and inserted an NG tube in one side of my nose to drain the bile from my stomach and a feeding tube in the other side of my nose to supply nutrition. The process was difficult, but after multiple attempts they were in place. Now I had four tubes in my body, which made all the days and nights long and full of misery.

I finally came home from the hospital three months later. Debbie had set up the living room as a medical crisis center! She had all the medical supplies we could ever need: dressings, ointments, alcohol prep, syringes, tubing, IV medications (antibiotics and TPN for nutrition), IV machines, and so on. If I had not been so pitiful, it would have been hilarious. During my time in Vanderbilt, I learned how to brush my teeth and shave with the help of my brother, Jerry. Thank you, man! I basically had to learn how to do everything all over again, and I'm still scared I'm going to fall going down steps. Necrotizing pancreatitis is a mean disease. Its main objective is to kill you, and, if you survive, it damages or destroys everything that was you. It hurts to admit it, but in many ways, I am not the same person I was and will never be that person again. Debbie and I have a good laugh sometimes because people always say how good I look. I know I should be grateful for looking better than I did in my emaciated pictures in 2016.

The only problem is that sometimes my feelings don't match my looks. I am a pretty good actor, and I try to put on a pleasant face when I am racked with pain, nausea, and sadness. I have fought "the good fight," and God has been good to me, but I still feel lost many moments of the day. I have tried to get back to being a good son, husband, and father. I've tried to rebuild our business, and Debbie and I have been blessed in that regard. During my rehabilitation, so many people stepped up that I can't begin to thank them all. Debbie's sister Denise was there almost daily, lending a shoulder to cry on, information, love, and support. She also received major points for bringing me fresh hot coffee each morning when she came to work! Frank Hannah kept our lawn mowed, performed other yard work, and organized donations. Other classmates paid our electric bills. Yvonne Kittrell set up a GoFundMe account, and thousands of dollars were donated. There are those good friends too numerous to count. I want to express my deepest gratitude to all who donated. It was a humbling experience to have to ask for help, but that seems to be the way God designed me. Whether I have been beaten down by my addiction or beaten by my health problems, I have had to ask for help. I don't fully know God's plan for me, but I know it includes spending time on my knees and crying out for God's help and mercy.

This last episode in 2016 left me unable to ask for help for quite a while. But God surrounded me with friends, family, and saints, who lifted up my family and me in prayer until I was able to help myself. Almost every day for the last three years, someone has said he or she has been praying for me, and I get emotional just thinking about that kind of love. My heart sometimes tells me I am not worthy of that kind of love and true friendship. I have been approached by strangers, asking whether I am Katlyn's dad or am I George Snodgrass? Katlyn documented our saga on Facebook and provided updates of my condition. That's why strangers I had never met recognized me. Whatever I think of the negative aspects of Facebook, I have now also experienced the positive effects. These people prayed for me to be healed. The prayer of a righteous person is powerful and produces results. Just look at me if you don't believe it!

During the last three years, I have been in the middle of a nightmare, due to chronic illness and watching everyone around me have to play a part. Watching the people you love go through your pain is maybe the hardest, most humbling part of it all. The chronic pain, nausea, depression, and fear of what will happen next have led me to thoughts of suicide. I can't honestly say that sad choice has never crossed my mind. Addicts who are using think a lot about suicide or not waking up. As the disease and life tear them down, they want relief. Chronic physical illness is the same way. I just want some relief, some easing of the pain and nausea, but then sometimes it doesn't come. I wake up another day, and it's like I am trapped in a never-ending episode of the *Twilight Zone*. My illness has a couple of different twists. I'll have a few hours of relief and think maybe it's going to get better and that there is hope this side of heaven. But then it comes again and slams me back into reality. Nevertheless, God gives me the faith and courage to face the dilemmas I have with my health.

I am being as honest as I can when I say that the challenges I face are not always easy. My purpose for writing this book is to encourage you to know that it is possible to make it through any situation. Most people don't have to go through the challenges I have endured. I am being completely transparent. Somebody needs you: your smile, your love, your compassion, your encouragement. I believe God has also saved *you* for a reason. But sometimes in this world you may have to walk through the fire.

In the spring of 2018, my case was presented to a panel of doctors at Vanderbilt, and a surgeon stated he was confident that he could correct my "issues" with surgery. However, it was a risk. I was so miserable and desperate for relief that I agreed to the surgery. About six weeks after surgery, he looked at Debbie and me and said he was not quite sure what he hooked up in my ductwork, but that he had made a mistake. Talk about a punch in the gut, literally! So many thoughts, so many feelings. At this point, I had a stent in my common bile duct to keep it open. My understanding was that if my stent wasn't removed after three to four months, it would most likely adhere to the wall of the duct and be difficult to remove. It had been in place almost six months, and I was still having "blockage" problems. I was referred by my internist to the Mayo Clinic in Florida. My stent had indeed adhered to the duct wall, and it took two procedures to safely remove it. The staff at the Mayo Clinic was an awesome group of medical professionals, and I have never been treated better. They had the courage to set aside their doctor-inspired egos and tell me there was nothing else they could do. Any further surgery would kill me. The stents were only causing more blockages, due to my anatomy.

As sick and sad as that made us feel, at least we finally had someone telling us that nothing more could be done. We could move on with our lives and end all the false hope. God, the Great Physician, was back in charge, fully in charge. He had been all along, but now I felt more at peace about it. We had done all we could do; now was the time to accept everything and move on with our lives. I am just trying to tell the truth about how I felt and what has been the soundtrack in my head. I have tried it all and have done it all. My daughter, Katlyn, called me a bad*** when writing about me for my birthday last year. I wish I could claim that title, but the truth is, when you are thrown in the deep end, you quickly learn how to be a good swimmer.

It sounds crazy, but with chronic illness, you learn how to be sick. What I mean is that you learn how to do what you have to do, to get through the day as comfortably as possible. And sometimes as you fight the battle, you think about just ending it, stopping the struggle. I am putting voice to something I know we have a hard time talking about: suicide, especially within the religious community. The journey of life is much harder for some of us than it is for others. Some of us have taken a few steps into Hades. But I hope and pray that if you ever think about giving up when negative thoughts consume you, you will remember my story, you will cry out to God for help, and you will find someone with whom to talk about it. (There is a resource list in the back of this book.) Sharing our struggles takes some of the power away from them. Again, I truly believe that God has brought you and me this far for a reason. I know that, as the Apostle Paul says in the Book of Philippians, "I can do all things through Christ who strengthens me," and that includes making it one more day carrying this overwhelming burden. I have hope now, and I know that everything is going to be all right in the end.

CHAPTER 17

It's a Wonderful Life

Every year Debbie and I plan a night a few days before Christmas Day to watch the classic movie *It's a Wonderful Life*. Even though we have seen it at least thirty-five times together, I always cry like a baby. For those who know me, that is not a big shock; I am an emotional person. The movie starts with Norman Rockwell scenes and values that remind me of my childhood. It doesn't take long for events to turn dark in the life of the main character, George Bailey, my alter ego. George's suicide attempt on the icy bridge is the emotional breaking point in his young life. Life has caught up with him, and he feels helpless and hopeless. I can relate to his story. Although most of my problems were self-induced and exacerbated by an out-of-control disease, both of us Georges feel like a child lost in the woods. We can't take it anymore, so we make a near-fatal decision. A final parallel to the movie was when all my friends through the GoFundMe account and numerous private donations came through for my family, just as George Bailey's friends did in the final scene. As his brother, Harry, declares in his toast, "George is the richest man in town," that was how I felt. God knows, I will never be the richest monetarily, but I feel like I am the richest when it comes to friends and having love and grace showered on me beyond my wildest dreams.

I had it all in my privileged life, and everything slowly went down the drain until I was totally empty. An addict is dead inside long before he takes his last breath. I thought I had been a leper to my family, a horrible human being who didn't deserve to live. The people around me did not deserve any more abuse from me. Thank God, I had that turn around when my dear father, through anger, finally cut me off from all my enablers—mainly, my mother. I finally had to reach out to my recovering friends and say that powerful word: *help.* I surrendered, and although I have relapsed and lost my way since that Christmas Eve of 1986, I have been able to say *help* again and again. I have received overflowing help and grace from the recovery community, the church, and my family. Through my active addiction and physical illness, I have been blessed beyond measure.

God has kept me around for a reason, to be His instrument when I allow it to happen. He has used my messed-up life to bless others and show them that if He can take a fallen man like me and use me for good, then He can do it in their lives. God has allowed me to stand on the mountaintop, and He has given me the free will to fall into dark valleys. Like George Bailey, I hope that as much as I tried to escape this world, I have been a blessing to those I have encountered. It is not me but Christ Who is alive and working in me. I know I am a miracle, and I know that it is truly better to give than to receive. I am thrilled at someone's birthday or Christmas as he or she prepares to open my gift. That excites me and fills me up like nothing else, and I get the same feeling when I am able to share my story of despair turned to hope. My talent and gift, all rolled into one, consist of what I have been through. If you can read or hear about me and doubt God, then I don't know what will convince you!

The worst part of what happened to me in 2016 was not being able to do my ministry. I thought I would never again be able to help others in a meaningful way, but God has restored me enough that I am really busier than ever, helping folks. New doors are opening, and unique opportunities are becoming available. My daughter, Katlyn, is helping me with my program, and that thrills me because I know it will continue and be in good hands. Please help those who ask for help and serve those in need. Show empathy and know that but for the grace of God, there *I* go! *You* could be the one asking for help.

Remember what Clarence the Angel said, "No man is a failure who has friends." So I must be the most successful man on earth because my friends are true friends. "A true friend is one walking in when others are walking out." Let's all go out there and be good friends to people in need. I promise they are praying and waiting for someone to walk into their lives. Please pray for all those who suffer, and pray for me as I try to serve. And don't forget, it's a wonderful life!! God bless!

Epilogue

Since in a large way my story started with my mother, I felt it only fitting to end it with her. My mother's life epitomizes the effects that addiction has on the family of an addict. My mother has never had a drink of alcohol or smoked a cigarette. I will never know how the addiction of the people she loves has affected her because she does not talk about it, due partly to denial and partly to embarrassment. Mama never really knew her father because of his alcoholism. She, at times, thought he was one of the farm hands who worked on the family farms throughout Wilson County. I don't know how much he was ever really in the same house with her.

Mama's brother Charles came along, representing the next generation of alcoholics. He was the first addict who caused trouble between my father and her. Mama was forced to deal with Charles and to protect her mother, Mama Julia. Daddy was not happy with Mama also trying to take care of my uncle. Then I came along, representing the next generation. Right in the middle of my parents' problems, I was sowing chaos and division in the family. I was destroying everything around me, including myself.

Self-centeredness is the common attribute of any using addict, and mine was full blown. I still talk to my mother today and pull things out of her that I did to her and Daddy. She told me recently that the hardest problem Daddy had with me was that he could not control me. I caused him more trouble than the wars he had fought on the other side of the world. I am also the only reason my parents considered splitting up.

Then along comes my beautiful nephew, Mama's grandbaby! He was truly the apple of her eye, but he had the genetic component that runs through our family on both sides: addiction. Satan raised his ugly head again and roared for more destruction. If it had not been for her Lord Jesus Christ, I don't know what my mother would have done.

This whole section is about my mother and her Savior, Jesus Christ! Her favorite hymn is "He Is My Everything." And he is! Since she was a little girl, Jesus has been part of her DNA. He lives in her and is everything she is about. I wish she had reached out for help from counselors or somebody. Ironically, she has probably talked to me more than anyone on earth about our family disease and how it has affected us all.

Mama has put up the good fight and has run the good race; she knows Who her Redeemer is. Her reward awaits her, and there will be no more pain breaking her heart as it has for more than ninety years! Her story will stand forever as a shining and powerful example of the power of love through her Deliverer Jesus Christ, to overcome all she has had to endure.

Resources

National Numbers

National Suicide Prevention Lifeline 1-800-273-8255

National Problem Gambling Helpline 800-522-4700

Cocaine Anonymous International Referral Line at 1-800-347-8998

Tennessee Numbers

Narcotics Anonymous 888-476-2482

Alcoholics Anonymous 615-831-1050

Cocaine Anonymous 901-725-5010

TN REDLINE 800-889-9789 Substance Abuse treatment and information line

TN Statewide Crisis line 855-274-7471

TN State Domestic Violence helpline 1-800-356-6767

Amazing Grace Recovery Program—www.amazingrp.org

     615-300-5269 615-868-3360

The Amazing Grace Recovery Program accepts donations so we can help more men and women who struggle with the disease of addiction. We are a nonprofit 503 (c) 3 organization. No gift is too small. Please send your contribution to:

The Amazing Grace Recovery Program
104 Medearis Drive
Old Hickory, TN 37138

Please visit our website for more information.

CPSIA information can be obtained
at www.ICGtesting.com
Printed in the USA
LVHW040718010520
654589LV00001B/1